FACTS

LEICESTER CITY

100 FACTS

LEICESTER CITY

Steve Horton

First published in Great Britain in 2020
by Wymer Publishing
www.wymerpublishing.co.uk
Wymer Publishing is a trading name of Wymer (UK) Ltd

First edition. Copyright © 2020 Steve Horton / Wymer Publishing.

ISBN 978-1-912782-47-5

Edited by Jerry Bloom.

The Author hereby asserts his rights to be identified
as the author of this work in accordance with sections
77 to 78 of the Copyright, Designs & Patents Act 1988.

All rights reserved. No part of this publication may be
reproduced or transmitted in any form or by any means,
electronic or mechanical, including photocopying, or any
information storage and retrieval system, without written
permission from the publisher.

This publication is sold subject to the condition that it shall not,
by way of trade or otherwise, be lent, re-sold, hired out or
otherwise circulated without the publishers prior consent in any
form of binding or cover other than that in which it is published
and without a similar condition including this condition
being imposed on the subsequent purchaser.

Typeset and Design by Andy Bishop / 1016 Sarpsborg
Printed and bound by CMP, Poole, Dorset

A catalogue record for this book is available from the British Library.

Sketches by Becky Welton. © 2014.

FACT 1
1884
LEICESTER FOSSE

Leicester City were founded in 1884 by a group of old school friends who named the new club Leicester Fosse.

The friends were former pupils of Wyggeston School and met at the home of Arthur Douglas Ashby. The house is still there at the corner of Fosse Road Central and King Richard's Road, hence the club being named Leicester Fosse. The Fosse Road was part of the ancient Fosse Way, a Roman road from Exeter to Lincoln.

The first manager, who combined the role with secretarial duties, was Ernest Marson. On 1st November 1884 the club played their first match, winning 5-1 against Syston Fosse at a private field off Fosse Road. The kit was black shirts with a blue diagonal stripe and white shorts.

The Fossils, as they soon became known, played eleven games that season. They won six, drew three and lost two. Another match against Syston Fosse was abandoned due to rain with the Fossils leading 1-0.

Leicester Fosse played friendlies for the first three seasons of their existence until they entered local cup competitions for the first time in 1887. They joined the Football Association in 1890 and the move to Filbert Street a year later was the catalyst for pushing for a place in the Football League.

FACT 2
1890 LEICESTERSHIRE COUNTY CUP WINNERS

Leicester Fosse won their first trophy in 1890. They beat Coalville 4-0 in a replay after the first game of the Leicestershire Challenge Cup final was drawn.

The two sides drew 1-1 at the Greyhound Ground in Loughborough on 5th April, in what the *Leicester Chronicle* described as a 'rough game'. The replay was arranged for the same venue a week later and attracted a crowd of 1,500.

There were few chances for either side in the first half. The Fossils' best chance came when a shot was tipped over the bar but the score remained goalless at halftime.

Early in the second half Fosse took the lead when Vickers scored from long range. Thompson scored the second and third goals, both of which were set up by Bentley. The fourth, shortly before the end, was from another long-range effort, this time by Jimmy Murdoch.

Fosse won the competition again in 1891, beating Gresley Rovers in the final. The competition is now known as the Leicestershire and Rutland Senior Cup and is contested by teams at non-league level.

FACT 3

1890
THE
FA CUP

When Leicester Fosse became a member of the Football Association in 1890, it allowed them entry into the qualifying rounds of the 1890-91 FA Cup.

In the first qualifying round Fosse were drawn at home to Burton Wanderers. It was a tough tie as their opponents had been in existence since 1871 and were competing in the Midland League.

Fosse were dealt a blow before the game at their Mill Lane ground when two of their half backs became unavailable. Wanderers took control of the game early on and scored within a few minutes of the kick-off. They continued to dominate and led 2-0 at halftime.

After the change of ends Fosse put up a good fight but couldn't find a way back into the game. Wanderers added a third to put the result beyond doubt and continued pressing to the end, adding another late on to complete a 4-0 win.

The *Leicester Mercury* was critical of the players selected to play in the forward line and reported that there was "an entire absence of coolness" in their play.

In the following round Wanderers were back in Leicestershire, where they were thrashed 8-1 by Loughborough.

FACT 4
1891 FILBERT STREET

After a nomadic existence which saw them have five homes in seven years, in 1891 Leicester Fosse moved to a new ground where they would remain for over a century.

Fosse thought they had finally found a home in 1889 when they developed Mill Lane, but after two seasons there the local Corporation soon reclaimed the land for redevelopment.

For the start of 1891-92, Fosse played at the Aylestone Road cricket ground while a new site was prepared. Local legend has it that the location was identified by the niece of Joseph Johnson, one of the founding members of the club.

The ground was initially called Walnut Street and it would be some time before Filbert Street became the preferred name instead. It was a simple ground, consisting of one wooden stand and three raised earth banks.

The first game at the new ground was on 17th October 1891 between the reserves and Melton Swifts. On 7th November the first team hosted a friendly against a Nottingham Forest XI.

Filbert Street remained the club's ground for 111 years and hosted almost 2,500 first team games prior to the move to what is now the King Power Stadium.

FACT 5

1891
MIDLAND
LEAGUE

Leicester Fosse's first season of league competition was 1891-92, but it was a disappointing campaign as they finished bottom of the table.

Fosse joined the Midland League and got off to a promising start, winning their first two games against Derby Junction and Grantham Rovers. However they were then brought crashing down with a 6-0 defeat at Burton Wanderers.

By the turn of the year the Fossils were near the bottom and had lost six out of their last seven games. They then gained a shock 4-1 win over title chasing Rotherham Town at Filbert Street, their biggest of the campaign.

The Rotherham win failed to prove a turning point and Fosse won just one of the remaining ten fixtures. Rotherham, who went on to finish top, humiliated Fosse 11-0 in the return fixture. Supporters didn't desert them however and the penultimate home game against Port Vale attracted the season's biggest crowd of 4,000.

Fosse finished the campaign as the league's bottom side, winning five of their twenty games and conceding 55 goals. It was a learning curve however and finishes of fourth and second in the next two campaigns were enough to put the club in contention for a place in the Football League.

FACT 6

1894
THE
FOOTBALL LEAGUE

Leicester Fosse were elected to the Football League for the 1894-95 season and had a creditable first campaign in the Second Division.

At the end of 1893-94 Northwich Victoria resigned from the Football League and Middlesbrough Ironopolis folded. This left just thirteen teams in the Second Division and Fosse, who had finished second in the Midland League, were elected along with Bury and Burton Wanderers.

The Fossils' first game was a 4-3 defeat at Grimsby Town, but the following week they overcame Rotherham Town 4-2 at Filbert Street.

They struggled for a while and their first victory was followed by four successive defeats, leaving them second from bottom. They began to pick up form though and gradually climbed the table.

On 15th January 1895 Fosse were hammered 8-2 at Darwen, but they then went unbeaten for their final thirteen games. They eventually finished fourth, only missing out on the promotion-relegation test matches on goal average.

Fosse had a great record at Filbert Street, winning nine successive games. These included a 9-1 thrashing of Walsall Town Swifts and 1-0 victory over runaway champions Bury. Away from home results were mixed but there were some good victories, most notably a 5-0 win at Burton Swifts.

FACT 7

1894 RECORD VICTORY

On 13th October 1894 Leicester Fosse thrashed Notts Olympic 13-0 in the FA Cup, a club record victory that still stands today.

Fosse were drawn away in this first qualifying round tie, but their Notts League opponents agreed a switch to Filbert Street to generate more revenue.

Fosse took an early lead through Skea, whose shot was fumbled by the keeper. Miller added a second then McArthur got the third with a long-range shot. McArthur added two more to make it 5-0 after just fifteen minutes.

The sixth and seventh goals came from Hill and Skea, who then completed his hat-trick with an unstoppable shot making it 8-0 at halftime.

For the ninth goal Miller's shot was saved by the hapless keeper who then stepped over the line with the ball. Within a minute Miller had taken it to double figures. The eleventh was a close-range effort from Hill and McArthur got the twelfth from a free kick.

Miller scored the thirteenth goal and it could have been fourteen had Skea's effort not been offside. The *Leicester Daily Post* described how "even the Fosse players began to tire at the monotony of the meeting".

The Fossils went on to beat Kimberley, Rushden and Loughborough to reach the first round proper, where they were beaten 4-1 at Bury.

FACT 8
1897
FIRST SENDING OFF

For the 35 years that the club was known as Leicester Fosse, only eight players were sent off. The first of these was Willie Freebairn against Lincoln City on 10th April 1897.

Freebairn, a right winger, had signed from Scottish side Abercorn the previous summer. He had an impressive start, scoring on his debut against Darwen but he did have a fiery temper.

In the match at Lincoln's Sincil Bank ground, the Fossils were trailing 2-1 when Freebairn was ordered off the pitch with ten minutes remaining. The *Lincolnshire Echo* reported that the home side had been the better team but Fosse were taking the defeat in "very bad spirit", with the sending off being for "insulting the linesman".

Early in 1898, Freebairn was suspended for a breach of club discipline and never played for Fosse again, returning to Scotland to play for East Stirling.

In October 1900 Freebairn was playing for Partick Thistle and received a kick in the chest, causing him to feel unwell for some time. On 18th November he was admitted to Glashow's Western Infirmary where he had an operation but complications set in and he died the following day aged just 26.

FACT 9

1908
PROMOTION TO
THE FIRST DIVISION

Leicester Fosse won promotion to the First Division in 1907-08 but left it late, only entering the top two by winning their final game.

The Fossils lost only once in their first ten games, but five of those were drawn. They then lost five from nine, meaning they were down in eighth place at the turn of the year.

A run of seven straight wins in February and March got Fosse back on track, but they then lost 5-1 at Fulham. Five games unbeaten followed to lift Fosse into third with one game left, their closest rivals having completed their fixtures.

Fosse knew a draw at Stoke on 27th April would be enough to secure promotion. Players and directors of Oldham, who would go up if Fosse lost, attended the game at the Victoria Ground. In a tight game in which every player gave their all, a first half goal from Tommy Shanks was all that separated the sides.

When the train carrying the Fosse players arrived back at 10:25pm, cheering crowds lined the streets as they were driven to a reception at the Grand Hotel. There, a band played *Conquering Heroes* as the players entered. The *Leicester Daily Post* reported that such scenes had not been seen in the city since the return of Boer War soldiers in 1902.

FACT 10
1908
OLYMPIAN & ENGLAND
INTERNATIONAL

Goalkeeper Horace Bailey was the first Leicester Fosse player to earn an England cap and he was also a gold medallist at the 1908 Olympics.

Bailey played for the Fossils as an amateur and was the first choice keeper for the promotion campaign of 1907-08. Away from football he was a ratings official for the Midland Railway.

In March 1908 Bailey was selected to play for England in a British Championship match in Cardiff, which they won 7-1. In the summer, he played in all four matches of a central European tour. England won all the games, scoring a total of 28 goals and conceding just two.

In October, Bailey was Great Britain's goalkeeper for the Olympic Games, which were held in London. They won the gold medal, beating Denmark 2-0 in the final and he conceded only one goal in the three games, in a 12-1 thrashing of Sweden.

After the games Bailey returned to the side but lost his place after a humiliating 12-0 defeat at Nottingham Forest the following April, even though the press said he played well. He made fifteen appearances in 1909-10 before moving to Derby County.

FACT 11
1909 RECORD DEFEAT

Leicester Fosse endured a miserable debut campaign in the top flight, finishing bottom of the table nine points from safety. They were already relegated by the time they suffered a humiliating 12-0 loss at Nottingham Forest on 21st April 1909.

This was Fosse's third from the last game of the season. Although their fate had been sealed, half of the First Division were still vulnerable to the second relegation spot, Forest being one of them.

The Fossils were 4-0 down after just fifteen minutes. They briefly rallied but couldn't find a way back into the game and conceded a penalty from which Forest scored a fifth. By halftime it was 8-0, Fosse's plight not helped by centre half James Gorman going off injured.

Fosse changed formation for the second half with the aim being one of damage limitation. Forest now had the wind in their favour and soon got a ninth goal. The tenth, eleventh and twelfth came in quick succession later in the half to complete what the *Leicester Daily Post* described as "a farcical absurd game".

Fosse's keeper was not to blame for any of the goals and the paper said it could easily have been twenty if he had been off form. It remains an all-time club record defeat.

FACT 12
1909
FRED SHINTON'S FIVE MINUTE HAT-TRICK

Leicester Fosse forward Fred Shinton scored a hat-trick within just five minutes in a game against Oldham Athletic on 20th November 1909.

In front of a crowd of 13,000, Oldham defended stubbornly and midway through the second half the game looked to be heading for a goalless draw. With twenty minutes to go, the visitors had a rare attack and Fosse keeper Horace Bailey had to be alert to tip a fierce drive onto the crossbar.

Fosse's forwards were galvanised into action by almost going behind. From their next attack, Threlfall put in a perfect cross from which Shinton scored with a powerful header. He soon added a second, winning possession and scoring with an opportunist shot that took the keeper by surprise.

By the time there were fifteen minutes to go Shinton had completed his hat-trick by nutmegging a defender before firing the ball into the corner of the net. There was no further scoring in the game and the Fossils were deserved winners.

This was Shinton's first hat-trick for Fosse since he was signed from West Bromwich Albion two years earlier. In 92 league games over two spells for the club, he scored an impressive 51 goals.

FACT 13
1915
RE-ELECTED TO
THE FOOTBALL LEAGUE

After finishing nineteenth in the Second Division in 1914-15, Leicester Fosse had to apply for re-election to the Football League. However by then football was the last thing from most people's minds.

When the season started on 2nd September 1914, Britain had been at war with Germany for a month and a huge armed forces recruitment drive was underway.

The Fossils avoided defeat in their first two games, both at home. They then lost six in succession and after dropping into the bottom two places in early November they remained there for the rest of the season.

Despite repeated calls to bring the season to a halt the Football League decided to carry on. Fosse's last game was a 2-0 defeat at Clapton Orient on 24th April. As the team set off by train for London, over 100 wounded soldiers arrived on another platform.

Fosse and bottom club had to apply for re-election to the Football League, along with four others hoping to gain entry at their expense. At the Annual General Meeting on 19th July, Fosse comfortably secured their place by getting 33 votes, more than anyone else.

Unsurprisingly, national competition was suspended for the duration of the war, but regional tournaments were allowed. When the Football League resumed in 1919, the club had a new name.

FACT 14
1919 LEICESTER CITY

The Football League resumed for the 1919-20 season with Leicester Fosse now known as Leicester City, following the liquidation of the original club.

Like many other clubs, the war hit Leicester Fosse financially and by the beginning of 1919 they owed the United Counties Bank over £3,000. At an Extraordinary General Meeting in May it was agreed to wind up the club and have it taken over by a new company, a move fully supported by the Football League. More investment in the team was promised, as well as renegotiation of the lease at Filbert Street.

Whilst the takeover process was ongoing, King George V visited Leicester and bestowed it City status. So at the beginning of July it was decided that the new start merited a new name and Leicester City was registered and ratified by the football authorities.

On 30th August Leicester City took on Wolverhampton Wanderers in the first Football League game at Filbert Street for over four years. City lost 2-1, but they went on to finish in a respectable fourteenth place at the end of the season.

FACT 15
1923
ARTHUR CHANDLER

Leicester City's all-time record scorer is Arthur Chandler, who joined the club from Queens Park Rangers in 1923.

Chandler was signed to bolster the attack of a side that had only narrowly missed out on promotion. In his debut season he got an impressive 24 goals, but City had to settle for a mid-table finish.

The following season, 1924-25, he formed a devastating partnership with Johnny Duncan that fired Leicester to promotion. They finished the season as champions and Chandler was the Second Division's leading scorer, finding the net 32 times.

Chandler wasn't daunted by the step up to the top-flight and scored 54 goals over the next two seasons. Despite now being in his thirties, he became even more prolific as City challenged for the title in 1928 and 1929, scoring 34 in each campaign. This included six in a 10-0 rout of Portsmouth on 20th October 1928.

In 1931-32 Chandler got 32 goals but his strike rate dropped over the next two seasons. Between 1932 and 1935 he was not a regular but his goals to game ratio was still respectable.

By the time Chandler left Leicester for Notts County in 1935 he was 39 years old and had scored 273 goals in 419 appearances in all competitions for City.

FACT 16

1924
JOHNNY DUNCAN
SCORES SIX

On Christmas Day 1924 Johnny Duncan scored six of Leicester City's goals as they hammered Port Vale 7-0 at Filbert Street.

Duncan joined Leicester from Raith Rovers in 1922. He could play in both midfield and attack and was the club's leading scorer in his first season.

In the Second Division fixture against Port Vale, it took Duncan 35 minutes to score his first goal. His goal doubled the lead that Arthur Chandler had given Leicester midway through the first half and three minutes later he added another to make it 3-0 at halftime.

By the time there had been just an hour of the game gone it was 6-0 thanks to Duncan's ability to get onto the pinpoint crossing of City's wingers. For an extended period after this Vale actually played reasonably well and were unlucky not to score in the second half when the ball stuck in the mud as it headed goalward.

Duncan also forced a number of good saves from the keeper and with three minutes remaining scored his sixth and Leicester's seventh.

Duncan left the club in 1930 but later returned as manager, guiding City to the FA Cup final in 1949.

FACT 17
1927
THE
DOUBLE DECKER

In 1927 Filbert Steet's capacity was expanded with the construction of the South Stand, commonly known as the 'Double Decker'.

Leicester City had now been at Filbert Street for 36 years but during that time the only changes to the ground had been the rebuilding of the Main Stand in 1921. With the club having won promotion in 1925, they were enjoying one of the best periods in their history and more spectator accommodation was needed.

The covered banking at the south end of the ground, known as the Spion Kop, was replaced with a two-tier stand. There were 5,500 seats on the upper tier and terracing below. The stand was almost a replica of one that had been built at West Ham United's Upton Park ground two years earlier.

Despite being formally called the South Stand, it was commonly known as the 'Double Decker'. The old Kop roof was put to good use, being moved to the north end of the ground.

Filbert Street's capacity was raised above 45,000 by the construction of the stand. It was open for the first time on 26th November for a match against league champions which City won 3-0.

FACT 18
1928 RECORD ATTENDANCE

The club's record attendance is 47,298, set when Tottenham Hotspur visited Filbert Street for an FA Cup 5th round tie on 18th February 1928.

City were riding high in the First Division and interest was huge as they aimed to reach the quarter finals of the FA Cup for only the second time. The *Sunday People* reported that the ground was besieged hours before the kick-off and gates were closed at 2pm with thousands still locked outside.

The first half was an end to end affair with chances for both sides. Johnny Duncan had City's best chance but hesitated whilst lining up his shot and allowed Spurs defenders to regain possession.

Two minutes after the restart some hesitation in Leicester's defence allowed Eugene O'Callaghan to put the visitors ahead. Eleven minutes later the same player scored again to double Tottenham's lead.

Leicester tried their best to get back into the game but Spurs were well organised in defence and easily repelled their attacks. In the closing stages Jimmy Dimmock skipped through the home defence to make it 3-0.

City had played very well and arguably had the greater share of play, but there could be no doubt Spurs had been clinical in attack as well as calm and composed in defence.

FACT 19
1929
RUNNERS UP AND
UNBEATEN AT HOME

Leicester enjoyed a great season in 1928-29, finishing second in the league and remaining unbeaten at Filbert Street.

The campaign got off to a mixed start with only one win from the first five games. Then during October, City won four games in succession, including a 10-0 thrashing of Portsmouth. This was one of nine occasions when they scored four or more goals at home.

At New Year, City were fifth in the table, but their away form prevented them from remaining serious championship contenders. On the road they lost twelve times and there were some heavy defeats, conceding five at both Derby and Bolton.

On 1st April City moved up to second place with a 4-1 home win over Aston Villa, who also had hopes of catching Sheffield Wednesday at the top of the table. However defeats that month to Villa and Portsmouth meant their chances of overhauling Wednesday remained slim.

In the penultimate game of the season City could only draw at Huddersfield, meaning Wednesday were champions. The following week they ended the season with a 6-1 win over Bolton at Filbert Street to secure runners up spot.

Despite the disappointment of missing out on the title, it had still been a memorable campaign in which 96 goals were scored, 43 of them by Arthur Chandler.

FACT 20

1930
LEICESTER CITY 6
ARSENAL 6

One of the most remarkable games Leicester City have been involved in was on 21st April 1930, when they drew 6-6 with Arsenal at Filbert Street.

The match was five days before Arsenal were due to face Huddersfield in the FA Cup final, meaning the Gunners rested a number of players. It was City's last home game of the season and there was a healthy Easter Monday crowd of over 27,000.

David Jack thought he had given Arsenal an early lead but his goal was ruled out for offside. The Gunners did then go ahead through Dave Halliday but City struck back to lead 3-1 at halftime thanks to two goals from Hugh Adcock and one from Arthur Lochhead.

In the first ten minutes of the second half Arsenal turned the game upside down. Cliff Bastin pulled one back then Halliday scored twice to stun City. Halliday got another to make it 5-3 but Ernie Hine pulled one back. Bastin then appeared to have sealed Arsenal's victory with his second.

Leicester refused to accept defeat though and goals from Len Barry and Arthur Chandler brought them level. It was a fantastic game and it remains the only occasion in English top-flight history that there has been a 6-6 score line.

FACT 21
1934
ARCHIE'S FOUR GOALS ON DEBUT

New signing Archie Gardiner scored four goals on his debut in 1934, but his Leicester City career did not continue in the same manner.

Twenty-year-old forward Gardiner was signed from Scottish side Heart of Midlothian, where he had mainly been a reserve. He went into City's side for the First Division game against Portsmouth at Fratton Park on 21st February 1934.

Gardiner scored twice in the first 25 minutes to give Leicester a 2-0 halftime lead. Ten minutes after the restart Gardiner completed his hat-trick, only for Portsmouth to hit back and score three quick goals to draw level. Leicester's lead was then restored by Gardiner and Danny Liddle got a late goal as it finished 5-3.

Two weeks later Gardiner got a hat-trick in a 4-1 home win over Arsenal. By the end of the season he had scored ten goals in sixteen appearances, but that was as good as it got for him with City.

Early in 1934-35 Gardiner fell out of favour with manager Arthur Lochhead and was sold to Wrexham. Although he scored a hat-trick on his debut there, he couldn't maintain his form and soon returned to Scotland, signing for Hamilton Academical.

FACT 22
1935
RELEGATED IN
JUBILEE SEASON

Leicester City celebrated their Golden Jubilee in 1934-35, but it was a season to forget as they were relegated to the Second Division.

Tragedy struck before the season began when manager Peter Hodge became seriously ill and resigned. He died in Scotland and six former and current players were pallbearers at his funeral.

City didn't start too well, with just one point from the opening three games. By New Year, they were bottom of the table and five successive defeats in January and February left them with a mountain to climb.

During the Spring, City won four games from five to give them some hope of staying up. A 2-2 draw with Grimsby in their penultimate home game lifted them out of the bottom two. However, they then lost 5-3 to Arsenal at Filbert Street and were leapfrogged by Middlesbrough who had a far better goal average.

On the last day of the season City had to win at Portsmouth and hope Middlesbrough lost to Chelsea. They got off to a disastrous start with defender Dai Jones scoring an own goal after five minutes. Although Gene O'Callaghan equalised late in the game it was never going to be enough as Middlesbrough had got the point they needed and City were down.

FACT 23
1935
RECORD APPEARANCE
HOLDER LEAVES

Adam Black, who made more league appearances for Leicester City than any other player, left the club following relegation in 1935.

Black established himself at right back after joining from Scottish side Bathgate in January 1920. He helped City to the Second Division title in 1925 and went on to captain the side. A consistent performer who was rarely injured, he was an ever present in five seasons.

Despite playing 528 league games over fifteen years for City, Black scored only four goals in that period. Three of these were penalties in 1924-25 and the other a freak sixty-yard free kick in 1933.

Black's Leicester career ended in disappointing fashion. With City battling relegation, the team was frequently changed and he was left out after a 2-0 defeat at Sunderland on 9th February. It was the 36-year olds last appearance for the club and he was allowed to leave on a free transfer at the end of the season.

Black retired from playing and remained in Leicester to become a newsagent. He died in 1981 at the age of 83 and a suite at the King Power Stadium is named after him.

FACT 24
1937
FROM RELEGATION ZONE TO PROMOTION

Leicester City finished as Second Division champions in 1936-37. Following a poor start, City brought in Frank Womack as manager in October 1936 and he lifted them from the relegation zone to the top of the table.

Just two games had been played when Arthur Lochhead resigned at the beginning of September, offering no explanation. For six weeks directors oversaw team selection, but results were poor and after ten games City were second from bottom. The board then acted quickly and they pulled off a major managerial coup, persuading Womack to leave First Division Grimsby Town for Filbert Street.

Womack set about turning things around with immediate effect. A 1-0 win in his first game in charge over Coventry City at Filbert Street was the start of an eleven game unbeaten run that lifted Leicester up to fifth by Christmas.

In February City won four games in succession to move into the top two, somewhere they would remain for the rest of the season. Promotion was secured on 24th April with a 2-1 home win over Nottingham Forest. The following week City secured the championship, beating Tottenham Hotspur 4-1 and leapfrogging Blackpool, who had completed their fixtures.

FACT 25
1939
RELEGATED

In 1938-39, Leicester City had a terrible second half of the season and won just three games after New Year. It meant they finished bottom of the First Division and were relegated.

City's results up to the end of December weren't great, but they picked up a number of draws and were sixteenth after beating Chelsea on New Year's Eve. Their form then dipped alarmingly, with just one win in nine games leaving them in the bottom two by the middle of March.

In the middle of April a win over Middlesbrough and a draw at Derby lifted City out of the bottom three with two games to play. However their fate was still out of their hands as the teams below them, Birmingham and Chelsea, had games in hand including one against each other.

On 24th April City's relegation was confirmed. In a cruel twist of fate they lost 2-0 at home to Grimsby Town, the club that manager Frank Womack had left to join them. In their final game, City lost 2-0 against Wolves at Filbert Street, meaning they finished bottom of the table. Womack resigned and was replaced by Tom Bromilow.

City had a reasonable start to 1939-40, winning two of their first three games, before the Football League was suspended at the outbreak of World War Two.

FACT 26
1940 FILBERT STREET BOMBED

In the early hours of 15th November 1940, Leicester City's Filbert Street ground was severely damaged when it was hit by a bomb dropped by the German Luftwaffe.

The city of Coventry was the main target that night, but a single bomber dropped seventeen bombs on Leicester as it was returning to Germany. Two people were killed and ten injured.

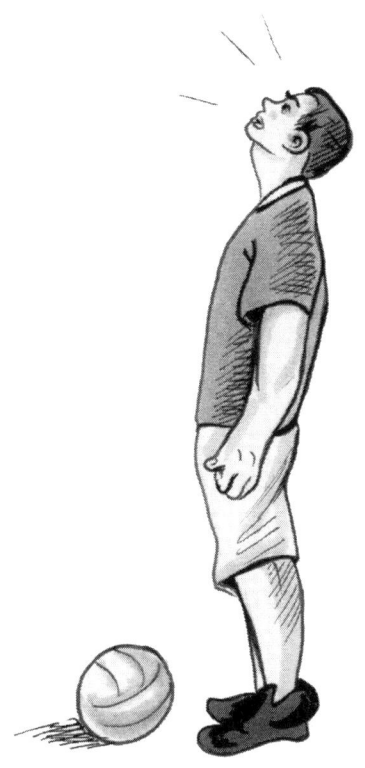

A 50kg device hit the Main Stand causing damage to the roof, boardroom, kitchens, toilets and gymnasium. The structure of the stand prevented any damage to neighbouring houses. Although strewn with debris, the pitch was not damaged.

City were already in financial trouble at the time and an application to the Football Association for a £15,000 loan to repair the damage was refused. In 1942 the stand was damaged again, this time by a fire which destroyed the dressing rooms and much of the seating. The boardroom and offices both suffered extensive water damage.

In an effort to generate other income during the war, the club hosted an R.A.F. boxing tournament and a baseball match involving American servicemen. By the time the Football League was ready to resume in 1946, City were glad just to be in business and any disappointment of relegation seven years earlier had been forgotten.

FACT 27
1941
THE
POST HORN GALLOP

In 1941 Leicester City's players took to the field to the sound of the *Post Horn Gallop*, something that remains a tradition to the present day.

The tune's origins lie in announcing the arrival of mail coaches in the 19th Century. At Filbert Street, it was played by a lone bugler wearing a long blue and white coat, as well as a top hat.

Even though sound technology and public address systems have improved over the years, any suggestion of making the tune louder or more modern have been resisted by the faithful. It continues to be played live by a bugler and despite being a difficult tune to play, it is unthinkable that it could simply be recorded once and played over the Tannoy.

The *Post Horn Gallop* is a stirring tune that gets the crowd ready for the game. It is arguably the oldest and most traditional tune that any team takes the pitch to. In the modern age, the *Post Horn Gallop* is not just for the stadium but used as a mobile ringtone by many fans.

FACT 28
1942 WAR LEAGUE SOUTH CHAMPIONS

There was success for Leicester City in 1941-42 when they finished as champions of the War League South.

The outbreak of the Second World War led to the suspension of the Football League. Regional competitions were set up for the remainder of the 1939-40 season and for the following campaign the leagues were set up into just north and south for those clubs who continued to seek fixtures.

City were one of thirteen clubs in the southern section and due to the uncertainties of who was available, guest players were allowed. However fixtures were very ad hoc and although City topped the table at the end of May, they had not played all the other teams home and away. Second placed West Bromwich Albion were six points behind but had played four games less.

For the next three seasons City only played in regional cup competitions with other Midlands clubs. In 1945-46 they did re-join the War League South, which was then far better structured. They played all 42 scheduled fixtures but results were disappointing and they finished third from bottom.

FACT 29

1948
THE
FOXES

In 1948 a fox was incorporated into Leicester City's club crest, leading to the nickname of the Foxes being adopted.

After the club's name was changed from Leicester Fosse to Leicester City in 1919, the nickname of the Fossils was dropped. Supporters and the press tended to refer to them as City or the Filberts.

For the 1948-49 season, City had an emblem on their shirts consisting of a fox in a shield. The fox is a representation of centuries of fox hunting tradition in the county of Leicestershire. Over the coming seasons, the nickname of the Foxes became widely used.

Over the years the crest has changed but the presence of a fox has remained a common theme. Sometimes it has said Leicester City Football Club, on others L.C.F.C. It has evolved from a shield to a circle and the current design, in use since the early 1990s, shows a fox's head rather than the whole body.

The club's mascot, Filbert the Fox, was introduced in 1992 and has attended every home game since. He has also worked hard in the community, visiting local schools, hospitals and community centres.

FACT 30
1949
LEICESTER CITY'S
FIRST FA CUP FINAL

When Leicester City reached the FA Cup final for the first time in 1949 they were still a Second Division club. However they were unable to upset the form book and were beaten by First Division Wolverhampton Wanderers.

In the semi-final, City had caused a sensational upset by beating Portsmouth, who were Football League champions that season. The Foxes were battling relegation from the Second Division and were clear underdogs for the final against Wolves, whose side contained a number of England internationals.

City's plight wasn't helped by keeper Ian McGraw being ruled out with a broken finger. They fell behind to a Jesse Pye header in the thirteenth minute but didn't buckle and continued to play well. Then three minutes before halftime they failed to clear a corner and Pye added another. Two minutes into the second half, Leicester were given hope when Mal Griffiths reacted quickest to score after Ken Chisholm's effort had been parried.

A few minutes after Griffiths' goal, Chisholm put the ball in the net but was ruled offside. With 25 minutes to go Sammy Smythe scored again for Wolves, ending City's hopes.

Despite the result, Leicester earned many plaudits for never giving up. They then turned their attention to league survival and escaped the drop to the Third Division by just one point.

FACT 31

1949
LONGEST SERVING PLAYER LEAVES

Leicester City's longest serving player was Sep Smith, who left the club in 1949 after nearly twenty years with the club.

Smith was just sixteen when he joined City in 1929, but had a disappointing debut in August that year when he replaced the injured Arthur Lochhead. Smith knuckled down in the reserves and was their leading scorer in 1930-31.

In 1931-32 Smith was given more first team opportunities, scoring eleven goals in 22 appearances. This was still not enough to make him a regular but the following season he was moved to right midfield and he blossomed, remaining in that position for the rest of his career.

In 1935 Smith gained his solitary England cap and the following year was appointed City's captain. His ability to pass on advice and tips to younger players was well respected.

The Second World War interrupted Smith's career and although he remained with the club, his 200+ appearances in wartime competition are not officially recognised. This means that when he retired from playing aged 37 at the end of 1948-49, he had made a total of 373 appearances for the club, scoring 37 goals.

In 2002 Smith was guest of honour for the last game at Filbert Street. When he died in 2006 aged 94, he was the oldest surviving England international.

FACT 32
1954
PROMOTION AFTER THREE-WAY BATTLE

Leicester City were promoted back to the First Division in 1953-54, finishing as champions after a thrilling three-way battle with Everton and Blackburn Rovers.

In their first game of 1954, City suffered a humiliating 7-1 defeat at Leeds United. This was the first of three successive defeats that saw them fall from first in the table to fifth. They managed to recover from this blip through and seven wins from eight took them back to the top.

On Good Friday, City were beaten 3-0 at Blackburn then could only draw with Notts County at Filbert Street the following day. This meant Blackburn led the table by a point from City with both teams having two games left. Everton were in third, a point behind City but with a game in hand.

On 19th April, City faced Blackburn at home. They knew that if they lost, then the visitors would be secured of promotion with the Foxes almost certainly missing out. In front of 40,054 fans City triumphed 4-0, meaning promotion was in their own hands with one game left.

Five days later City won 3-1 at already relegated Brentford to secure their top flight return. They went up as champions, finishing above Everton on goal average and a point ahead of Blackburn.

FACT 33

1955
STRAIGHT
BACK DOWN

Unfortunately following the promotion season the club was relegated straight back to the Second Division in 1954-55, with a leaky defence proving their downfall.

Just one win from their first eight games set the tone for City's season. They had few problems finding the net but at the back they just couldn't stop conceding. It was not until Portsmouth were beaten 4-0 at Filbert Street in the 31st game that they finally kept a clean sheet.

High scoring defeats included a 6-4 loss at West Bromwich Albion, 5-0 at Tottenham and 5-0 at Wolves. There were some big wins too, with City hitting four or more goals on five occasions. When the season ended, they had scored 74 but conceded 86.

City's Leading scorer was Arthur Rowley, but his respectable return of 23 goals from 37 games was still nowhere near as prolific as he had been managing in the Second Division. Halfway through the season City paid Lincoln a club record £27,500 fee for striker Andy Graver to try and add to their firepower. He failed to live up to expectations and was sold back to Lincoln at the end of the season.

Relegation was confirmed in City's penultimate game, a 3-1 defeat at Huddersfield Town. They finished the season in 21st place, two points adrift of safety.

FACT 34

1955
TELEVISION AT FILBERT STREET

The first-time television cameras recorded the action at Filbert Street was on 12th November 1955, when Leicester City beat Swansea Town 6-1 in a Second Division fixture.

The game was recorded for highlights to be shown on BBC TV, with David Coleman providing the commentary. The visitors were top of the league, with City languishing in thirteenth.

City started the game well and twice went close to scoring before Mal Griffiths made it 1-0 after twelve minutes. The rest of the first half was a cagey affair, with Swansea rarely threatening to get back into the game.

Swansea began the second half well but the Foxes defence stood firm. Willie Gardiner then made it 2-0 after 56 minutes and Derek Hogg set up Johnny Morris for the third after an hour. In a devastating nine minute spell, Gardiner got two more to complete a hat-trick and Arthur Rowley added the sixth. Swansea's consolation came two minutes from time and it finished 6-1.

The big victory was the start of a turnaround in fortunes for City, who eventually finished fifth. Ironically, in the return fixture at the Vetch Field Swansea ran out 6-1 winners.

FACT 35
1957
PROMOTION WITH
GOALS GALORE

Leicester City won promotion back to the First Division in 1956-57, scoring a club record 109 goals. 44 of those were scored by Arthur Rowley, the best ever individual tally at the club.

With Dave Halliday as manager, the Foxes lost just once in their opening ten games. They went top with a 5-4 win at Bury in their ninth game and were never out of the promotion places all season. They hit five or more goals on nine occasions, the biggest wins being 7-2 over Bristol Rovers and 6-0 against Blackburn.

Twelve games unbeaten between December and February saw City stretch their lead at the top and it became only a matter of when not if they would secure promotion.

On 6th April, Rowley scored a first half hat-trick as City beat West Ham 5-3 to ensure First Division football the following season. It took them past the century mark in terms of goals scored, and Rowley surpassed his own goals per season record.

There were still four games remaining and City took their final tally to 109. Rowley, who played in all 42 league games, added one more to finish with 44, beating his own club record of 41, set in 1952-53.

FACT 36
1957
FLOODLIGHTS

The first game to take place under floodlights at Filbert Street was on 23rd October 1957 when Leicester City played a friendly against Borussia Dortmund.

Filbert Street's floodlights were installed during the close season at a cost of £25,000. For their inauguration a prestige friendly was arranged against Borussia Dortmund, winners of the last two West German national championships.

The attendance of 18,398 was much lower than expected, but they witnessed a fine showing by City. In the first half defences reigned supreme, but after the break the Foxes gained the upper hand. Eddie Russell and Don Walker were dominant in midfield and Dortmund keeper Heinz Kwiatowski saved brilliantly from Ian McNeill and Willie Gardiner.

After an hour, a perfect cross from Derek Hogg evaded two defenders allowing Gardiner to score the only goal of the game from close range. Hogg was outstanding all game, running the full back Burgsmuller ragged.

Further floodlit friendlies were staged that season against BSK Beograd of Yugoslavia and Brazilians Canto de Rio. The following summer, City travelled to Dortmund for a return match, which the Germans won 2-1.

FACT 37

1958
APPOINTMENT OF
MATT GILLIES

Leicester City's longest serving manager, Matt Gillies, was appointed in November 1958.

Scotsman Gillies played for City from 1952 to 1955. He took a short break after retiring from playing, then returned to Filbert Street as a coach in 1956. In November 1958, with City bottom of the First Division, the club parted company with Dave Halliday and appointed Gillies as manager.

City avoided relegation with Gillies in charge, then saw gradual season on season improvement. In 1961 they finished sixth and reached the FA Cup final. Gillies made some shrewd signings, most notably future England World Cup winner Gordon Banks from Chesterfield and promoted promising youngsters like Frank McLintock to the first team.

In 1963 City went close to becoming First Division champions and appeared in a second FA Cup final in three years. The following year they won their first major trophy, the League Cup.

The sale of Frank McLintock saw City struggle in 1964-65, but Gillies invested the money shrewdly, bringing in Derek Dougan and Jackie Sinclair. Successive top eight finishes followed, but in January 1968 he was forced to take a break after developing tuberculosis.

When Gillies returned to take over the side, results were poor and he resigned in November 1968. He was in charge for ten years and 21 days, making him City's longest serving manager.

FACT 38

1961
FA CUP
FINALISTS

The Foxes reached the FA Cup final for the second time in 1961. However they were unable to prevent Tottenham Hotspur becoming the first club in the 20th Century to win the Double of League Championship and FA Cup.

Leicester's run to the final saw them face First Division opposition only once, when they overcame Birmingham City in the fifth round. They had enjoyed a respectable league season, finishing sixth, but Spurs were the favourites for the final having already secured the league title.

The opening fifteen minutes was fairly evenly matched, but Leicester had a terrible blow midway through the first half when full back Len Chalmers picked up an injury. He battled on but Spurs were able to take advantage of this and took control of the game, having a 38th minute goal ruled out for offside.

In the 66th minute Bobby Smith scored with a shot that gave Gordon Banks in the Leicester goal no chance. With fifteen minutes remaining Smith set up Terry Dyson who headed Spurs into a 2-0 lead. Soon after this Chalmers left the field, meaning Leicester finished with ten men.

Most newspapers felt Leicester had been unlucky due to Chalmers being injured with no substitutes allowed. However it remained debatable whether they could have overcome Spurs even if he was fully fit.

FACT 39

1961
INTO
EUROPE

Leicester City competed in European competition for the first time in 1961-62. However their run in the European Cup Winners Cup was short lived and they were eliminated by Atletico Madrid, who went on to win the trophy.

The Foxes were England's representatives in the competition due to Tottenham having won the Double and competing in the European Champions Cup.

In the preliminary round City were drawn against Glenavon of Northern Ireland. Despite falling behind in the first leg in Belfast, the Foxes fought back to comfortably win 4-1. They then completed the job with a 3-1 victory at Filbert Street.

The task in the first round was much harder as City were paired with Atletico Madrid. In front of over 25,000 at Filbert Street on 25th October, Ken Keyworth put City ahead after 56 minutes, but Atletico took control of the tie thanks to a late equaliser by Mendonca.

Three weeks later at the Metropolitan Stadium in Madrid, Leicester were second best throughout against a team riding high in the Spanish league. They held out for an hour, but when Richard Norman handled in the area, Collar converted the spot kick. With twelve minutes remaining Jones secured the victory for Atletico, who went on to beat Fiorentina in the final.

FACT 40

1963 ICE KINGS

Leicester City were known as the 'Ice Kings' in 1962-63 when a twelve-game unbeaten run during an extremely harsh winter took them to the top of the table.

The worst winter in 200 years saw temperatures plummet to minus twenty and all First Division fixtures in January were postponed. The freezing conditions continued throughout February but City had been able to make the Filbert Street pitch playable using fertiliser, weed killer and burning oil drums.

On 9th February City beat Arsenal 2-0 at home, their first league fixture since a 5-1 Boxing Day victory over Leyton Orient. They won their next five matches, the winning run finally coming to an end on 23rd March when they drew 2-2 with Tottenham at Filbert Street.

On 8th April a 1-1 draw at Blackpool took the Foxes to the top of the table, but they were then beaten 2-0 at West Ham. They then had a 4-3 home win over Manchester United to go back to the top with just five games to go.

The title destiny was still not in City's hands as they needed both Everton and Tottenham, who were both a point behind with a game in hand, to slip up. However it was City who collapsed as they lost four of those last five games to eventually finish fourth.

FACT 41
1963
FAVOURITES CITY
LOSE FA CUP FINAL

Leicester City lost their second FA Cup final in three years in 1963, despite being favourites to beat Manchester United.

In the league the Foxes had twice beaten United, who only narrowly avoided relegation. City had reached Wembley thanks to a 1-0 victory over Liverpool in the semi-final, a game in which Gordon Banks was immense in goal.

In the first fifteen minutes City were the better side and only frantic United defending kept them out. It was then United's turn to attack and Banks made some good saves, before Denis Law put them 1-0 up after half an hour.

Early in the second half Graham Cross missed a golden opportunity to equalise when he shot wide. In the 57th minute David Herd made it 2-0 to United after Banks could only parry Bobby Charlton's shot.

United remained in control of the game but Frank McLintock pulled one back with ten minutes remaining. It only galvanised United more, with Law hitting the post before Banks fumbled a cross into the path of Herd, who put United 3-1 ahead with just five minutes left.

After the game Leicester's captain Colin Appleton offered no excuses, telling reporters they had underperformed and that he couldn't understand how United had finished so low in the league.

FACT 42

1964 LEAGUE CUP WINNERS

The first major trophy came in 1964 with victory in the League Cup, beating Stoke City over two legs in the final.

This was the fourth season of the League Cup, the final of which was initially played over two legs rather than at Wembley. The Foxes had beaten Aldershot, Tranmere, Gillingham, Norwich and West Ham to reach the final.

For the first leg at Stoke's Victoria Ground on 15th April, Leicester were up against it for an hour and it was no surprise when Stoke took a 1-0 lead. Leicester remained on the back foot but got a fortunate equaliser when a poor clearance fell into the path of Dave Gibson, who skilfully lobbed the keeper to leave things finely balanced.

A week later at Filbert Street, Mike Stringfellow scored for Leicester after just six minutes, but Stoke equalised through Dennis Viollet. In the second half the visitors were reduced to ten men through injury and Leicester took advantage, Dave Gibson scoring twice to put them 3-1 ahead.

To their credit Stoke kept plugging away and George Kinnell scored to make it a nervy finish. Gordon Banks was solid in goal though and Leicester held on for victory and claimed their first major trophy.

FACT 43
1965 LEAGUE CUP FINALISTS

Leicester City reached the League Cup final again in 1965 but they were unable to retain the trophy, losing to Chelsea.

The Foxes enjoyed a straightforward run as they sought to become the first team to retain the League Cup. All of their ties were against lower division sides and they had some big wins, beating Grimsby 5-0 and thrashing Coventry 8-1 away from home in the quarter final.

First Division Chelsea awaited in the final, with the first leg at Stamford Bridge on 15th March. Leicester were 1-0 down at halftime but in the first minute of the second half Colin Appleton equalised.

Terry Venables restored Chelsea's lead from the penalty spot but with fifteen minutes remaining Jimmy Goodfellow levelled the scores again. Eddie McCreadie scored another for Chelsea ten minutes from time and the game finished 3-2.

At Filbert Street on 5th April title chasing Chelsea were well organised and prevented City from mounting any sustained spells of pressure. At the other end, Gordon Banks was called into action more than his Chelsea counterpart Peter Bonetti.

The game finished 0-0, meaning that as well as not retaining the trophy City missed out on European football the following season. This was the first occasion when the League Cup winners went into the Fairs Cup (later UEFA Cup and Europa League).

FACT 44
1966
WORLD CUP WINNER & BALLON D'OR NOMINEE

In 1966 Leicester City's goalkeeper Gordon Banks was a member of England's World Cup winning side. He was then nominated for the Ballon D'Or, awarded annually by the magazine *France Football* to the world's best player.

Banks had played just 26 games for Chesterfield when Matt Gillies paid £7,000 for him before the 1959-60 season. By the end of the campaign he had replaced Scottish international Johnny Anderson as the club's number one.

In the 1963 FA Cup semi-final City beat Liverpool 1-0. Banks later said it was his finest club performance and the *News of the World* reported that City had one shot, compared to Liverpool's 34.

Banks made his England debut in 1963 and was the undisputed first choice keeper by the time of the World Cup, held on home soil in 1966. He did not concede a goal until the semi-final when Portugal scored a late penalty. He was not at fault for either of the two goals conceded in the final against West Germany, which England won 4-2.

After being nominated for the Ballon D'Or, Banks finished fourteenth in the vote which was won by England teammate Bobby Charlton. However within a year of winning the World Cup he had lost his place to Peter Shilton, and was sold to Stoke City in April 1967.

FACT 45
1967
GOALKEEPER
PETER SHILTON SCORES

Leicester City were so sure of teenage goalkeeper Peter Shilton's potential that in April 1967 they made him first choice keeper aged just seventeen and sold Gordon Banks. Six months later, Shilton even managed to score a goal himself.

The match against Southampton at The Dell was just four weeks after Shilton's eighteenth birthday. The home side scored first but Mike Stringfellow equalised shortly before halftime.

In the second half City took control and were 4-1 up when Shilton sent a long punt upfield. Southampton's keeper misjudged the bounce and it went into the net. Shilton didn't realise he had scored until afterwards, as it had been a misty day.

Despite displacing Banks at Leicester, Shilton had to be patient when it came to taking over as England number one. His first cap came against East Germany in 1970, the first of 125 in an international career spanning twenty years.

Shilton left Leicester in 1974, joining Stoke City for £325,000 which was then a world record for a goalkeeper. He continued playing professionally until the age of 47, making 1,005 league appearances for eight different clubs.

FACT 46
1968 ZAMBIA TOUR

One of the more unusual destinations that Leicester City have visited was in 1968 when they undertook a post season tour of Zambia.

City had been invited, along with an FA delegation, to the newly independent country which was preparing for their first entries into the World Cup and Africa Cup of Nations. The party remained there for three weeks, playing six matches in total.

In their final game City beat the Zambian national side 3-2, but there were chaotic scenes when a member of the crowd attacked an English linesman. The players left the pitch as rocks were hurled from the terraces.

Despite the sad end to the tour, City secretary Alf Pallett had been impressed at the efforts of those charged with developing the game in the country. After returning home, he received a letter from President Kenneth Kaunda which said, "I am taking special note of the observations that you made and I am sure they will help us develop our soccer performances. I am glad that you were able to come and do so much help for us in this field."

The following year when City reached the FA Cup final they received a telegram from Zambia's sports minister wishing them good luck.

FACT 47
1968
BREAKING THE BRITISH TRANSFER RECORD

In the summer of 1968 Leicester City smashed the British transfer record when they signed striker Alan Clarke from Fulham. However he stayed at the Foxes for just a year before moving on for another record fee.

Clarke was a month short of his 22nd birthday when City paid Fulham £150,000 for his services. He had scored 45 goals in 86 games for the Cottagers but they weren't enough to save them from relegation in 1967-68. The fee smashed the previous record of £115,000 which Manchester United paid Torino for Denis Law in 1962.

In City's second home game Clarke scored a hat-trick in a 3-0 win over champions Manchester City. However with City fighting relegation, he was often criticised for "going missing" in games. He did star in the FA Cup though, scoring the winning goal in the semi-final against West Bromwich Albion.

The season ended with City as beaten cup finalists and relegated to the Second Division. Don Revie's Leeds United, newly crowned champions, then broke the transfer record again, paying £165,000 to take him to Elland Road.

FACT 48
1969
AN UNWANTED DOUBLE

In 1968-69 Leicester City completed an unwanted double, losing the FA Cup final as well as being relegated from the First Division.

In the league, the Foxes failed to win successive games all season and endured some heavy defeats, including a 7-1 thrashing at Everton. In the cup, they caused a fifth round upset by beating Liverpool 1-0 in a replay at Anfield, before going on to knock out holders West Bromwich Albion in the semi-final.

The cup final against the previous season's league champions Manchester City took place on 26th April. Despite being the underdogs, Leicester gave a good showing and only Neil Young's 24th minute goal separated the sides at halftime. Both sides had their chances after the break but there was no further scoring, with Leicester forward Alan Clarke being named man of the match.

Despite the final disappointment, Leicester still had five league games in their bid to avoid relegation. They got vital home wins over Tottenham and Sunderland but lost at Ipswich. A 1-1 draw with Everton at Filbert Street in their penultimate game meant only victory against Manchester United at Old Trafford three days later would be enough. Despite gallant effort, they lost 3-2 and were back in the Second Division for the first time in twelve years.

FACT 49
1971
MEANEST DEFENCE WINS PROMOTION

Leicester City won promotion back to the First Division in 1970-71, thanks partly to conceding fewer goals than on any other occasion in their history.

Despite losing their first game, City soon found form and were top of the table by the end of September following four straight wins. They were still there at Christmas, but three defeats in a row saw them drop out of the promotion places and at one stage they were as low as seventh.

After a 4-1 home defeat to Birmingham City on 16th January, the Foxes remained unbeaten in the league for the rest of the season. A 1-0 win over Sheffield Wednesday at Filbert Street on 10th March took them back into the top two and they didn't fall back out of it.

Promotion, along with the championship, were secured in the penultimate game of the season when Alistair Brown's last minute goal was enough to beat Bristol City at Ashton Gate.

During their unbeaten run of seventeen games, City conceded just four goals. Their end of season tally of just thirty goals conceded is an all-time club record.

FACT 50
1971 CHARITY SHIELD WINNERS

Leicester City were the surprising winners of the Charity Shield in 1971, after Double winners Arsenal and other potential contenders declined to take part.

When Arsenal opted to fulfil a contractual obligation to face Dutch giants Feyenoord in a friendly in Rotterdam, it left the FA with a headache for the traditional curtain raiser to the season. Cup finalists Liverpool did agree to participate but their Anfield ground was unavailable due to building work.

Ground redevelopment also ruled out league runners up Leeds, while League Cup winners Tottenham were touring Scotland. The FA turned to Second Division champions Leicester, with the game taking place at Filbert Street.

In front of 25,104 on a hot sunny day, young right back Steve Whitworth scored the only goal of the game after fifteen minutes, tapping the ball into the net after a goalmouth scramble. It turned out to be his only goal for the club in a career that went on to span over 350 games.

City put in an excellent performance against Liverpool, who were one of the favourites for the league title. Jimmy Bloomfield's players had shown that the forthcoming season needn't be one of simply fighting for survival. They went on to finish a respectable twelfth in the league.

FACT 51
1972
FRANK WORTHINGTON ARRIVES

When Liverpool backed out of a deal to sign Frank Worthington due to his high blood pressure, Leicester City took a chance on him and he became a big crowd favourite at Filbert Street.

A flair player, Worthington became one of the stars of Jimmy Bloomfield's free flowing side. Although he had a reputation for partying and womanising off the pitch, he never let this interfere with his ability to perform on matchdays. Liverpool may have been concerned about his health, but in five full seasons at City he was an ever present twice and missed no more than three games in each of the others.

Worthington's performances for the Foxes in 1973-74, when he scored 24 goals in all competitions, earned him a call up to the England squad. He got eight caps that year, six of them under Joe Mercer's management. However after playing twice for new manager Don Revie, he was never picked again.

Worthington scored a total of 78 goals in 239 appearances for City. Early in the 1977-78 season Bloomfield's successor Frank McLintock allowed him to leave. He dropped a division to join Bolton but helped them to promotion in a season that City went down.

1975
FACT 52 GRAHAM CROSS'S 600TH AND LAST APPEARANCE

Leicester City's record appearance holder in all competitions is Graham Cross, whose 600th appearance on 23rd August 1975 turned out to be his last.

Cross joined the Foxes from school and scored on his reserve team debut when he was just fifteen. In April 1961 he made his senior debut whilst aged seventeen and scored in that as well, but he didn't become a regular in the side in 1962-63.

Initially the versatile Cross was used in midfield or attack but he soon settled in the centre of defence. He continued to have great energy and contributed to attacks, scoring 37 goals over the course of his career.

In total, Cross made 597 starts for City, and came on as a substitute three times to take his total to 600 if the 1971 Charity Shield against Liverpool is taken into account. Nobody has played more times for City, although his record of 498 games in the league is bettered by Adam Black, who managed 528.

Cross made two appearances early in the 1975-76 season, but lost his place to Jeff Blockley. His last game for City was a 3-0 defeat at Newcastle. Towards the end of the season he was loaned to Chesterfield and then signed for Brighton in the summer of 1976.

FACT 53
1975
EIGHTEEN WINLESS GAMES

Leicester City's longest run of games without a league win is eighteen, spread over two seasons in the mid 1970s.

On 9th April 1975 the Foxes beat Middlesbrough 1-0 at Filbert Street, their third successive win. They then picked up just one point from their remaining three games of the season without even scoring a goal. They Finished in eighteenth place, three points ahead of the final relegation spot.

The 1975-76 season saw City draw six and lose one of their first seven games. This meant they were seventeenth in the table, but three successive defeats saw them fall into the relegation zone.

City then had three more draws in a row before losing 3-2 at home to Tottenham. Their eighteenth successive game without a win was a 1-1 draw at Goodison Park, although it did lift them out of the bottom three.

On 8th November 1975 the Foxes finally won a game, beating Burnley 3-2 at Filbert Street. In the next game the revival continued with a 2-1 at Sheffield United and this was followed by two draws and two wins.

City continued to progress for the rest of the season and by losing just once in their final eleven games, they finished in seventh place, something that was unthinkable in November.

FACT 54
1977
JIMMY BLOOMFIELD LEAVES

One of Leicester City's most popular managers was Jimmy Bloomfield, who left the club in 1977 after six years in charge.

Bloomfield's side played some of the most entertaining football ever seen at Filbert Street. Players such as Alan Birchenall and Frank Worthington were firm crowd favourites and the side gelled both on and off the pitch. They played free flowing attacking football that earned plaudits nationwide.

On the training ground, Bloomfield loved to join in the five a side games. He rarely shouted and preferred to put an arm around the shoulder to get the best out of players, as shown with his man management of Worthington.

Bloomfield sent his sides out to entertain and Birchenall recalled years later that he would prefer to lose 4-3 and play well, rather than 1-0 and play badly. Results were mixed, but City's games were never dull. During his time in charge the closest they came to success was reaching the FA Cup semi-final in 1974, but they lost to Liverpool.

In May 1977, after the side had begun to break up, Bloomfield resigned as manager, returning to his former club Orient. He died of cancer in 1983 at the age of just 49.

FACT 55
1978
DISMAL SEASON
ENDS IN RELEGATION

Following the departure of Jimmy Bloomfield, Frank McLintock returned to Leicester City as manager. However he was sacked before the end of a season that saw City finish bottom of the table with just five wins from 42 games.

City were unbeaten for their first three games, winning one and drawing two. They then lost five in succession to drop into the relegation zone at the end of September, where they remained all season.

The main problem was in attack, where Frank Worthington was not adequately replaced. The previous season he had been top scorer with fourteen goals, but this time around joint top marksmen Roger Davies and Mark Goodwin managed just four each. City only won five league games all season and went out of both cups to lower division opposition.

At the beginning of April, McLintock left by mutual consent and Ian McFarlane took temporary charge. On the 15th of the month, the Foxes lost 4-1 at home to Birmingham City, confirming their fate with four games still to play.

For most of the season City and Newcastle had been swapping places at the bottom of the table. In the final game at Filbert Street, City beat Newcastle 3-0 to draw level on 22 points but remained bottom due to an inferior goal difference.

FACT 56
1979
LEICESTER CITY'S YOUNGEST GOALSCORER

The youngest player to score for Leicester City is Dave Buchanan. He was just 16 years and 192 days old when he found the net against Oldham Athletic at Filbert Street on New Year's Day 1979.

Britain was in the midst of an Arctic blast and this was one of only two fixtures to go ahead in the whole of the Football League. The extreme weather meant there was a lower than average crowd of just 12,757.

City hadn't won for seven games and Buchanan was one of two teenagers given debuts by manager Jock Wallace. Buchanan had signed for the club the previous summer from non-league Loughborough Dynamo.

Despite the icy conditions City played their best football of the season. Midway through the first half Buchanan scored the opening goal, cleverly lobbing the keeper after being set up by Tommy Williams. Bobby Smith made it 2-0 shortly before halftime.

Buchanan finished the season with five goals from nineteen league appearances. However he failed to keep the momentum going and he played fourteen more times for the club before signing for Peterborough in 1983.

The other teenager Buchanan made his debut alongside — Gary Lineker — had a far different career path. Buchanan remains City's youngest ever scorer, but his record as youngest player was broken in 2005 by Ashley Chambers.

FACT 57

1979
KEITH WELLER LEAVES

One of Leicester City's greatest players, Keith Weller, left the club in 1979.

City paid £100,000 to Chelsea for Weller in September 1971 and he became an influential player in Jimmy Boomfield's entertaining side. He could play both as an attacking midfielder and on the wing, possessing great pace and an explosive shot.

In August 1972 he hit a memorable hat-trick in a 3-2 win over Liverpool at Filbert Street. In 1974, he scored what was later voted City's greatest ever goal in a 4-0 win over Luton Town in the FA Cup. At the end of that season he played four games for England while Joe Mercer was interim manager, but he didn't get another international opportunity after Don Revie was appointed.

Towards the end of his City career Weller struggled with his knees, but he remained at the club following relegation in 1978. In an FA Cup tie against Norwich City on an icy day in January 1979, he famously donned white tights under his shorts. He was mercilessly ribbed by opposition fans but answered back with a goal in the 3-0 victory.

After that Norwich game, Weller played just once more for City. After 43 goals in 297 appearances he joined New England Tea Men and settled in the United States, where he died of cancer in 2004.

FACT 58
1980 FA CUP GIANT KILLING

Leicester City were the victims of an FA Cup giant killing act in 1980, when they were beaten 1-0 by Harlow Town in a third round replay.

City were firm favourites to progress past the Isthmian League side, who had already played seven ties that season. In front of 21,302 fans at Filbert Street Martin Henderson gave City the lead midway through the first half. However despite dominating the rest of the game, the visitors stayed solid at the back. With a minute remaining the Foxes were stunned when retail worker Neil Prosser broke clear and equalised.

Four days later the sides met again in front of over 9,000 at Harlow's Sports Centre ground. City were never allowed to settle by a side consisting of a number of physical training instructors.

City fell behind after 42 minutes and could have gone 2-0 down in the second half had it not been for a goal line clearance by Mark Goodwin. For the last fifteen minutes City threw everything at Harlow, but the home side held on.

It was the first time City had been beaten by a non-league side since 1914-15, when there were only two divisions. Manager Jock Wallace offered no excuses, saying "They kept it tight at the back and took their chance when it came".

FACT 59
1980
PROMOTED
AS CHAMPIONS

Leicester City overcame their FA Cup shock at Harlow to clinch promotion in 1979-80, going back up as champions of the Second Division.

A 1-0 win over Newcastle United took the Foxes to the top of the table at the beginning of February. However they failed to win any of their next five matches and dropped out of the promotion places. They hit back with two straight wins to move up to second, then suffered a shock home loss to Preston.

City hit form at just the right time in April. They won four games in succession, including victories over promotion rivals Chelsea and Birmingham City. This took them to the top of the table with just three games remaining, although only one point separated the top four sides so there was no room for error.

In their penultimate game City beat already relegated Charlton 2-1 at Filbert Street while Chelsea could only draw at Swansea. Due to their vastly superior goal difference only a freak combination of results could stop them going up now.

On 3rd May, City made no mistake by beating Orient 1-0 at Brisbane Road, meaning they went up as champions.

FACT 60
RELEGATED DESPITE ENDING LIVERPOOL RUN

Although Leicester City were relegated in 1980-81, they did have the honour of becoming the first side to beat Liverpool at Anfield for three years.

The Foxes rarely looked like avoiding the drop and from the beginning of November were never out of the bottom three. Defeat at Brighton on 20th April effectively sealed their fate with two games left.

The one highlight of a torrid season was at Anfield on 31st January 1981. Liverpool, champions in 1979 and 1980, had been unbeaten at home for their previous 85 games in all competitions, a record that stretched back to 21st January 1978. The Foxes had lost their last five games without scoring a goal and been dumped out of the FA Cup in midweek by Third Division Exeter City.

At halftime things were going as predicted, as City trailed to Alan Young's fifteenth minute own goal. However early in the second half an uncharacteristic mistake by Liverpool keeper Ray Clemence allowed Pat Byrne to equalise. With fifteen minutes remaining Jim Melrose scored from long range to give City the lead.

For the remainder of the game City were up against it and there were four minutes added time, unheard of then. However they held on for a famous victory, but it failed to inspire them to escape the drop.

FACT 61
1982
THREE KEEPERS
IN ONE GAME

When Leicester City goalkeeper Mark Wallington's run of seven years without missing a game came to an end, his replacement failed to see out the game.

The run of 331 consecutive appearances began on 4th January 1975 and finally came to an end on 6th March 1982. City were leading 1-0 at home to Shrewsbury Town in the FA Cup sixth round when Wallington injured his thigh in the 21st minute. With no substitute keepers he remained on the pitch but was at fault for both goals as the Shrews quickly hit back to lead 2-1.

It was clear Wallington could not continue and City's one substitute Jim Melrose came on, with Alan Young going in goal. City were level before halftime thanks to an own goal by Steve Biggins.

Early in the second half, Young picked up an injury when he fell awkwardly, leading to Steve Lynex going in goal. However after treatment on the sidelines Young was fit to go back between the sticks, with Lynex going back on the wing. City eventually won 5-2 in a game that needed thirteen minutes of injury time.

The following week Wallington was replaced in goal by teenager Nicky Walker. In 1982-83 Wallington was an ever present again but left the club in 1985 to join Derby County.

FACT 62
1983
A CONTROVERSIAL PROMOTION

Leicester City were promoted in controversial circumstances in 1983. On the last day of the season a game in which their closest rivals were losing was abandoned with a few minutes to go, but the result was allowed to stand and City's promotion was confirmed.

By the final day of the season, QPR and Wolves had already secured First Division football for the following campaign. City knew a win at home to relegation threatened Burnley would guarantee promotion, but if they slipped up Fulham could go back above them. In an added twist, Fulham were away to City's East Midlands rivals Derby County, who needed a point themselves to avoid relegation.

City struggled to break down a dogged Burnley defence and could only draw 0-0. At the Baseball Ground, Fulham fell behind in the 71st minute and the game was played out in chaotic scenes as the crowd encroached towards the pitch. After 88 minutes and the score still 1-0, the referee blew the whistle for offside, leading to a pitch invasion. It was impossible to clear the fans and the game was declared over.

Fulham appealed to the Football League to replay the game and had the support of City manager Gordon Milne. However the result was allowed to stand and City were promoted.

FACT 63
1984 CENTENARY CELEBRATIONS

Leicester City celebrated their centenary in 1984 with a gathering of ex-players and friendly against Aberdeen, managed by a young Sir Alex Ferguson.

The match with Aberdeen was part of City's pre-season preparations and took place on 13th August 1984. A game between former players was a precursor to the main event that saw City take on a side that had won a league and cup double in Scotland the previous season.

City dominated the first half and were awarded a 38th minute penalty when Tommy McQueen was fouled in the box. Steve Lynex stepped up to convert the kick and they remained in the lead at halftime.

Aberdeen were the better side in the second half and had a chance to equalise from the penalty spot. However Eric Black's kick rebounded off the post and the follow up was skied over the bar. Black did make amends though with an equaliser twenty minutes from time and the game finished 1-1.

Afterwards, City manager Gordon Milne was complimentary of the Aberdeen side, saying "They produced just the sort of standard of football we were expecting, it was a far better test for us."

Aberdeen went on to win the league again in 1985 and the cup in 1986, prompting Manchester United to appoint Ferguson as their manager.

FACT 64
1985
GARY LINEKER LEAVES

After finishing the season as the First Division joint leading scorer in 1984-85, Gary Lineker left Leicester City and signed for champions Everton.

Lineker was eighteen years old when he made his debut against Charlton Athletic on New Year's Day, 1979 but was mainly a squad player for the next two and a half seasons.

In 1981-82 Lineker established himself in the side, playing in a more central role. The following season he scored 26 goals as City won promotion back to the top-flight.

Lineker was not daunted by playing at a higher level and he formed a devastating partnership with Alan Smith. In 1983-84 his 22 goals was second only to Liverpool's Ian Rush. 1984-85 was even better as he hit 24, sharing the top scorer mantle with Chelsea's Kerry Dixon.

City had still struggled in the league and finished just two points above the relegation places in 1984-85. It was inevitable that bigger clubs would want Lineker and an £800,000 deal was agreed for him to join champions Everton.

Lineker went on to play for Barcelona and Tottenham before ending his career in Japan. Leicester City are still his first love and he led a consortium to take over the club when its existence was threatened in 2002. He is an honorary vice-president and a freeman of the city.

1987
FACT 65
15 SUCCESSIVE AWAY DEFEATS & RELEGATION

Leicester City were relegated in 1986-87, fifteen successive away defeats being key to their downfall.

After ten games City were ninth in the table. However a 2-0 loss at Charlton Athletic was the first of eight games without a win that saw them drop into the bottom three.

At Filbert Street City had some good wins, including a 6-1 thrashing of Sheffield Wednesday. However on the road they were awful and that defeat at Charlton was the first of fifteen away defeats in a row, seventeen if FA and League Cup ties are taken into account.

If City were to have any hope of staying up, they had to break the sequence on the last day of the season. They travelled to Oxford United needing to better Charlton's result. Even if they could do that, they still faced promotion/relegation playoffs with three sides from the Second Division.

With 25 minutes to go Oxford were reduced to ten men when Dean Saunders was sent off. Despite this City were unable to find a winner against a side who still needed a point themselves to ensure safety. The game ended 0-0 and Leicester were down, although as Charlton beat QPR, even a victory for the Foxes wouldn't have been enough due to their inferior goal difference.

FACT 66

1991
BRIAN LITTLE APPOINTED MANAGER

Brian Little was appointed as Leicester City's manager in 1991. He immediately turned around the club's fortunes but his eventual departure was controversial.

City were lucky to avoid relegation in 1990-1991. They finished third from bottom but league restructuring meant just two teams were relegated from the Second Division.

Manager David Pleat had been sacked in January, with Gordon Lee taking over on a temporary basis. At the end of May City appointed Little, who had taken Darlington from non-league to the Third Division in successive seasons.

Little didn't make wholesale changes, but under him City made a great start, winning four of their first five games. They eventually finished fourth but lost the playoff final.

In 1992-93 City lost the playoff final again before finally gaining promotion the following year. With a limited budget City were expected to struggle and it was no surprise when they lost their opening two fixtures to Premier League title hopefuls Newcastle and Blackburn.

Despite City's league position, Little's managerial stock remained high but he departed in contentious circumstances. In early November Ron Atkinson was sacked by fellow strugglers Aston Villa, where Little had spent his whole playing career. Leicester refused an approach but were furious when Little resigned and was appointed at Villa just three days later.

FACT 67
1992
MISSING OUT ON THE FIRST PREMIER LEAGUE

Leicester City missed out on the chance to become founder members of the Premier League in 1992 when they were beaten in the Second Division playoff final.

For the 1992-93 season top flight clubs were to break away to form the Premier League, allowing them to share television revenues between themselves. City looked set to go up automatically into the new set-up after five straight wins in April took them into second place. However they lost their final two games and had to settle for a place in the playoffs.

After drawing 1-1 at Cambridge United in the first leg of the semi-final, City had an emphatic 5-0 win at Filbert Street. This set up a final at Wembley against Blackburn Rovers. They had spent big in their bid to make the top-flight and also installed Kenny Daglish, three times a title winner with Liverpool, as manager.

Shortly before halftime City fell behind when Mike Newell converted a spot kick. In the second half City conceded another penalty when keeper Carl Muggleton brought down Mark Atkins. Newell stepped forward again, but Muggleton made amends and saved the kick.

City were unable to find a way back and had to settle for another year in the second tier, renamed as the First Division of the Football League.

FACT 68
1993
SECOND SUCCESSIVE PLAYOFF FINAL DEFEAT

Leicester City missed out on the Premier League again in 1993, losing a thrilling playoff final 4-3 to Swindon Town.

Unlike in 1991-92, City never looked like going up automatically. They finished in sixth place, twenty points behind champions Newcastle United, who thrashed them 7-1 at St James Park on the last day of the regular season.

In the first leg of the semi-final against Portsmouth, Julian Joachim's goal four minutes from time was all that separated the sides. Goals from Ian Ormondroyd and Steve Thompson earned the Foxes a 2-2 draw at Fratton Park to take them to Wembley.

Swindon's player-manager Glenn Hoddle gave his side a 42nd minute lead, then early in the second half Craig Maskell put them 2-0 up. Shaun Taylor's 53rd minute goal looked to have settled the game, but Joachim scored four minutes later to give City a lifeline.

Two goals in two minutes midway through the half from Steve Walsh and Steve Thompson drew Leicester level. With six minutes remaining, City's players were furious when the referee adjudged Kevin Poole to have fouled Steve White in the area. Paul Bodin converted the penalty meaning City's comeback was in vain.

For the second year in a row City had lost the playoff final to a debatable penalty. It also meant they had lost on each of their six visits to Wembley Stadium.

FACT 69
1993
THE
CARLING STAND

Filbert Street underwent major renovation in 1993 with the building of a massive new main stand.

With all stadiums in the top two divisions needing to become all seated following the Hillsborough Disaster, City needed to make a decision on their future home. Bolting seats onto existing terraces would have left a capacity of 17,000 and with no suitable sites for a new stadium, the only option was to expand the one side of Filbert Street where there was room.

A ten year sponsorship deal was agreed with the Carling Brewery and the new two tier 9,300 seat stand also contained 28 executive boxes. It was fully operational by December that year and brought the ground capacity up to 22,517 all seated.

The new stand allowed Filbert Street to become a seven day a week operation, bringing in revenues through conferences and exhibitions. Conference suites were named after club legends Gordon Banks and Gary Lineker, with a link to the early history being made with the Fosse restaurant.

Filbert Street's proximity to the M1 made it an attractive proposition for hospitality and for these purposes it was rebranded as the City Business Stadium.

FACT 70
1994
THIRD TIME LUCKY
IN THE PLAYOFFS

Leicester City finally made it to the Premier League in 1994, winning the playoff final at the third attempt.

The Foxes were second in the table in the middle of March but three successive defeats saw them fall into the playoff places. They eventually finished fourth, ten points behind second placed Nottingham Forest.

In the semi-final City faced Tranmere Rovers. After a 0-0 draw in the first leg at Prenton Park, a late goal from David Speedie gave City a 2-1 win at Filbert Street. Their opponents in their third successive Wembley playoff final at Wembley were East Midlands rivals Derby County.

Shortly before the half hour mark City fell behind when Tommy Johnson scored for Derby. However four minutes before halftime Steve Walsh converted Gary Coatsworth's cross to equalise. Derby players were furious and felt their keeper was impeded, but the goal was allowed to stand.

For much of the second half Leicester were up against it, but their five man defence stood firm. With just six minutes to go, Ian Ormondroyd's header could only be parried by the Derby keeper. The ball fell into the path of Walsh who made no mistake to score his second of the game and take City into the Premier League.

FACT 71

1995
STRAIGHT
BACK DOWN

Leicester City's first season in the Premier League was a forgettable one in which they never looked like avoiding relegation.

Pundits predicted before the start of the season that City would struggle. Their task was also made harder by the fact league restructuring would mean four clubs went down instead of the usual three.

The Foxes picked up just one point from their opening five games. They then got their first win in style, beating a Tottenham side containing German World Cup winner Jürgen Klinsmann 3-1.

From the end of October, the Foxes were never out of the relegation zone. When Brian Little left to manage Aston Villa, Mark McGhee replaced him but was unable to halt the slide.

Over the course of the season City won just six out of 42 games. Their longest unbeaten run of three games came after relegation had been confirmed with five still to play. They ended the season with 29 points, leaving them nineteen from safety. Despite such a disappointing campaign, the board retained faith in McGhee for the 1995-96 season.

FACT 72
1996
LAST GASP PLAYOFF VICTORY

In 1995-96 Leicester City were promoted back to the Premier League, thanks to Steve Claridge's late, late goal in the playoff final at Wembley.

At the beginning of December City were second in the table when manager Mark McGhee stunned the club by resigning to take over at struggling Wolves. Despite them being in a precarious position, he felt they had better long-term potential than City.

Martin O'Neill took over and although results were mixed initially, he steered the Foxes to a playoff spot. In the semi-final against Stoke they drew 0-0 at Filbert Street then Garry Parker's goal in the second leg at the Victoria Ground was enough to take City into a Wembley final with Crystal Palace.

Palace led at halftime but with fifteen minutes to go City's persistence was rewarded when they were given a penalty after Muzzy Izzet was tripped up in the area. Gary Parker converted the kick to take the game into extra time.

With penalties looming, O'Neill replaced first choice keeper Kevin Poole with Zelijko Kalac, who he felt was better equipped to save spot kicks as he was six feet seven inches tall. However he wasn't needed as when Palace failed to clear a free kick, Claridge scored from outside the area with just two seconds remaining and City were back in the Premier League.

FACT 73
1997
WINNERS OF THE LAST REPLAYED FINAL

Leicester City won the League Cup in 1996-97, beating Middlesbrough in the last time a domestic cup final was decided by a replay.

In the first game at Wembley Martin O'Neill's game plan was to nullify the threat of Middlesbrough's foreign stars. This was largely successful and Kasey Keller in goal had little to do. City's best chance in normal time fell to Emile Heskey, but his header bounced back off the bar.

Five minutes into extra time City fell behind to a goal by Fabrizio Ravanelli. Middlesbrough's players were more fit but they couldn't extend their lead. With two minutes to go Heskey equalised, getting to the ball quickest after his header came off the bar.

In the replay at Hillsborough in Sheffield, City again stifled Middlesbrough's flair with Pontus Kamark doing an excellent man marking job on Juninho. It was 0-0 after ninety minutes with Middlesbrough's fans taunting City with chants of "boring, boring Leicester".

The Foxes started extra time as the better side and after ten minutes Steve Claridge volleyed the ball home after a Steve Walsh knock down. City were made to sweat for their victory. Keller saved well from Craig Hignett and Ravanelli shot just wide, but they held out to win their first trophy since 1964.

FACT 74
1997 UEFA CUP

When Leicester City played in European club competition for the first time in 36 years, they were knocked out by the same side that had beaten them in 1961.

The Foxes were drawn against Atletico Madrid in the first round of the UEFA Cup. In the first leg, 3,000 City fans in the Manzanares Stadium were in dreamland when Ian Marshall gave them an eleventh minute lead. They held out until the seventieth minute when Juninho levelled the scores.

Within a minute City fell behind to a controversial penalty that was converted by Christian Vieri. Keeper Kasey Keller made a number of good saves to keep the score at 2-1 as Leicester's players tired late on.

With away goals counting double, City were hopeful of turning the tie around in the second leg by using the compact Filbert Street to their advantage. In an emotionally charged atmosphere, City were on top in the first half. Muzzy Izzet and Neil Lennon were solid in midfield and Atletico were constantly worried by the presence of Emile Heskey.

Early in the second half both sides were reduced to ten men, with City's Garry Parker harshly seeing red for taking a free kick too quickly. As in the first leg, Atletico's superior quality and they went on to win 2-0 with goals from Juninho and Kiko.

FACT 75

1998
DON'T GO MARTIN

When manager Martin O'Neill looked set for talks on taking over at Leeds United in the 1998-99 season, he was convinced to stay at Filbert Street by fan power.

At the beginning of October Leeds were looking for a new manager and O'Neill soon became their number one choice. This led to the board having to issue a "hands off" warning three times in a week.

On 13th October, O'Neill announced that he would like the opportunity to talk to Leeds and believed a gentleman's agreement enabled him to do so. Leicester denied this, but O'Neill stopped short of forcing the issue by resigning and the situation was left in limbo.

On 19th October, City played Spurs at Filbert Street. Thousands of fans held up signs saying, "Don't Go Martin" and his name was sung loudly. City won 2-1 thanks to a stunning volley from Muzzy Izzet and goal from Emile Heskey.

After the game, nobody knew if this had been O'Neill's farewell. However two days later he called a press conference to announce he would be staying, saying the reaction of the fans played a large part in this decision.

FACT 76
1999
INJURY TIME
HEARTBREAK AT WEMBLEY

There was heartbreak upon reaching the League Cup final in 1999 but losing 1-0 to Tottenham Hotspur, whose winning goal came in injury time.

On a drab day, there was little to brighten things up in the first half. The closest either side came to scoring came when City's Emile Heskey was in the clear after being set up by Neil Lennon, only for Ramon Vega to get back and make a last ditch tackle as he lined up his shot.

Early in the second half Robert Ullathorne's shot was spilled by Spurs' keeper Ian Walker, but he just got to the ball as Tony Cottee followed in for the rebound.

With half an hour remaining Spurs were reduced to ten men when Justin Edinburgh reacted angrily to a Robbie Savage challenge. The Foxes were unable to capitalise on this though. Heskey was struggling after a recent injury lay off and was replaced by Ian Marshall.

The game suddenly came to life in the last five minutes. Cottee missed from an acute angle and Kasey Keller saved a long-range effort from Darren Anderton. In injury time Stefan Iversen's shot was only parried by Keller into the path of Allan Nielsen, who stooped to head the ball home and break Leicester's hearts.

FACT 77
2000
WINNING LAST WEMBLEY LEAGUE CUP FINAL

In 2000 Leicester City made up for the disappointment of losing the previous season's League Cup final by winning the competition for the third time.

The Foxes' opponents at Wembley were Tranmere Rovers. With the famous old stadium set to be rebuilt, this was the last League Cup final to be played there.

Tranmere had more of the opening play, but apart from one shot that Tim Flowers tipped round the post they created few clear chances. Flowers also dealt easily with their long throw specialist Dave Challinor.

After half an hour, Matt Elliot headed City into the lead. In the 55th minute Muzzy Izzet had a great chance to make it 2-0, but he miscontrolled and Tranmere scrambled the ball clear.

Rovers were reduced to ten men with thirty minutes left when Clint Hill was sent off. City failed to capitalise though and were rocked when Dave Kelly equalised with twelve minutes to go. Just three minutes later, Leicester's nerves were calmed when Elliot headed them back ahead.

Leicester were up against it in the closing stages and had a scare when Rovers hit the bar. They had always seemed to be playing within themselves however and there was no doubting that they were deserved winners when the final whistle went.

FACT 78

2000
EMILE HESKEY LEAVES FOR CLUB RECORD FEE

Emile Heskey, a local boy made good, left Leicester City in March 2000. The £11 million transfer fee from Liverpool was the highest the club had received for a player at the time.

Heskey came through the youth ranks and was just seventeen years old when he made his debut at QPR in March 1995 during an injury crisis. He signed his first professional contract that summer and was soon in the first team, scoring seven goals in thirty appearances as the Foxes won promotion.

In 1996-97 Heskey was second to David Beckham as Young Player of the Year. He scored ten goals and was a handful to opposition defenders due to his pace, strong build and shooting ability. He was not an out and out goal scorer but his presence drew defenders away from teammates, allowing them space to take chances.

Liverpool manager Gerard Houllier was an admirer of Heskey, who won his first international caps for England in 1999. Once City had won the League Cup in 2000, Liverpool made an £11 million bid, which was too much for Leicester to turn down.

Heskey spent four and a half years at Liverpool but he didn't forget the club that developed him. When Leicester's existence was threatened in 2000, Heskey donated to Gary Lineker's consortium that took over the club.

FACT 79
2001
EIGHT CONSECUTIVE DEFEATS

Leicester City's worst losing sequence was in 2000-01 when they lost eight games in succession.

With Martin O'Neill leaving to manage Celtic, Peter Taylor took over as manager. The Foxes remained unbeaten for the first eight games and a 0-0 draw at Sunderland on 1st October put them top of the table.

Defeats to Manchester United and Liverpool then saw them fall to fifth, but City's home form kept them in the top half of the table. A 2-0 win over Liverpool on 3rd March saw them move up to fourth. However the following week they were stunned in the 6th round of the FA Cup when Wycombe Wanderers of the Third Division won 2-1 at Filbert Street.

When the Foxes returned to league action, they had three successive away games, all of which were lost. They were then beaten at home by struggling Coventry and Manchester City, both of whom went on to be relegated.

A 2-0 defeat at Derby County was followed by a 3-0 home loss to Middlesbrough. The eighth successive defeat was at St James Park, where Newcastle United beat the Foxes 1-0.

The losing run was finally ended in the penultimate game, a 4-2 win over Tottenham at Filbert Street. The season ended with a 3-1 defeat at Leeds, meaning City finished a disappointing thirteenth.

FACT 80

2002
RELEGATED LAST SEASON
AT FILBERT STREET

Leicester City's final season at Filbert Street in 2001-02 ended in relegation from the Premier League.

The club needed a larger stadium to compete at the top level but expansion of the existing ground was unviable due to two sides backing on to terraced housing.

Sadly the last season at the old ground was a disappointing one. A 5-0 defeat at home to newly promoted Bolton Wanderers on the opening day set the tone and this was followed by a 4-0 loss at Arsenal.

City were already relegated by the final day of the season, but there was still a carnival atmosphere to bring 111 years of football at the old ground to an end. Club legends including Frank Worthington, Alan Birchenall and Gary Lineker were presented to the crowd, who were determined to enjoy the occasion.

Spurs looked to have spoiled the party when Teddy Sheringham scored a 54th minute penalty. However City fought back and Paul Dickov equalised after an hour. With twenty minutes remaining, Matthew Piper headed his first goal for the club to send the home fans wild. At the end of the game, the celebratory atmosphere was such that nobody would have believed City had been relegated.

FACT 81

2002
THE
WALKERS STADIUM

When Leicester City moved from Filbert Street to their new stadium, there was controversy over the proposed name.

The new 32,000 seat stadium at Freeman's Wharf was a short distance from Filbert Street and cost £35 million to build. It was not surprising when a naming rights deal was announced, but the proposed Walkers Bowl was not popular.

After a torrent of online complaints, mainly to do with the name being corporate, American and tacky due to the bowl of crisps analogy, the club agreed to a rethink. After consultation between club and sponsors, the Walkers Stadium was agreed upon.

The stadium, which had taken just a year to build, was opened on 23rd July 2002. Gary Lineker arrived in a Walkers lorry and used a giant pair of scissors to cut the ribbon.

On 4th August the first game took place there as City drew 1-1 with Athletic Bilbao in a friendly. Six days later, Brian Deane scored both goals as City beat Watford 2-0 in the first competitive game, watched by a capacity crowd.

After nine years as the Walkers Stadium, the naming rights changed again in 2011 when it became the King Power Stadium.

FACT 82
2003
PROMOTION DESPITE FINANCIAL DIFFICULTIES

Leicester City overcame entering Administration in 2002 to finish second in the table and gain promotion to the Premier League.

The collapse of ITV Digital was a huge blow to all clubs outside the Premier League, as it meant expected television monies failed to arrive. Already burdened with players on higher salaries and the cost of the new stadium, City went into Administration in October 2002 with debts of over £30 million.

Despite having to offload some players and an embargo on incoming transfers, City were never out of the top two from the beginning of November. Manager Micky Adams, who took over towards the end of the previous season, was able to keep the players' minds focused clearly on the pitch and they lost just twice after the turn of the year.

The club's future was secured in February 2003 when a consortium led by former legendary player Gary Lineker took control. Promotion was secured with three games to spare on 19th April, when City beat Brighton 2-0 before 31,909 fans at the Walkers Stadium. City finished the season with 92 points, twelve more than third place Sheffield United.

FACT 83

2004
STRAIGHT BACK
DOWN AGAIN

For the fifth time in their history, Leicester City were relegated from the top-flight in their first season after being promoted.

Money for transfers remained minimal and Micky Adams had to rely on free agents in the battle to establish City in the top flight. He brought in plenty of experience, but some players were past their prime.

The Foxes didn't win until their fifth game, an impressive 4-0 victory over Leeds United. However they then lost five games in a row. Four games unbeaten in November lifted them into twelfth, but after that it was all downhill.

Between December and the middle of March City didn't win in thirteen matches, including successive 4-0 and 5-0 home defeats against Chelsea and Aston Villa respectively. The run finally came to an end with a win at Birmingham but this only lifted them out of the relegation zone for two weeks.

Four successive defeats in April took City to the brink and a 2-2 draw at Charlton on 1st May confirmed their fate with two games remaining. Adams remained at the club but after a poor start to the following season he resigned.

FACT 84
2005 TWO ABANDONED MATCHES

Travelling Leicester City fans were out of luck not once but twice in 2005 when away games at both Burnley and Plymouth were abandoned.

The game at Burnley on New Year's Day was abandoned after nineteen minutes due to torrential rain making the pitch unplayable. The score was 0-0 with each side only managing one chance due to the conditions.

City manager Craig Levein was supportive of the decision, telling reporters "It was a good decision for it had become a bit of a lottery. It was just a matter of time before someone got injured and that is clearly not an acceptable situation. The referee was right to give it a go but it became unplayable." The game was replayed on 8th March and ended in a 0-0 draw.

On 2nd November City made the long journey to Plymouth Argyle on a Wednesday night. They were trailing 1-0 at halftime when the referee called the game to a halt due to a waterlogged pitch. Fans who made the long trip had already been to Cardiff and Preston in the last eight days. When the game was replayed the following March, City were unable to take advantage, losing 1-0.

FACT 85
2005
A SCHOOLBOY PLAYER

The youngest player to appear for Leicester City is Ashley Chambers, who was just fifteen years and 203 days when he came off the bench in a League Cup tie against Blackpool on 20th September 2005.

Chambers, a speedy striker, was born and raised in Leicester and had been on the club's books since he was eight years old. He made his first appearance for the reserves a few days after his fifteenth birthday in March 2005 and played for England at junior level.

In this League Cup tie at home to Blackpool, City were leading 2-1 when Chambers was brought on as an injury time substitute to run the clock down.

It was the only appearance that Chambers made that season and in 2006-07 a cruciate ligament injury curtailed his progress. During 2007-08 and 2008-09 he did make eight more appearances. However he started only one of those games, against West Bromwich Albion in December 2007, in which he himself was substituted.

After loan spells with Wycombe Wanderers and Grimsby Town, Chambers agreed a permanent deal with York City in November 2010.

FACT 86
2006
A GOAL IN NINE SECONDS

The quickest goal by a Leicester City player came on 15th April 2006 when Matty Fryatt scored after just nine seconds against Preston North End.

City went straight into attack in this game at the King Power, with Fryatt turning in a cross from Gareth Williams in club record time. However they were unable to build on this lead and playoff chasing Preston drew level on the stroke of halftime.

Despite being urged by manager Rob Kelly to have another fast start in the second half, the Foxes were behind just five minutes after it kicked off. There was no further scoring in the game, watched by 21,865 fans.

Although City lost this game, Fryatt's contribution was later recognised when he was named by the BBC as the club's key player for the season. Since arriving from Walsall in January, he had scored six goals to help them pull away from the relegation zone.

Fryatt remained at the King Power until 2011 when he joined Hull City. He retired from playing in 2017 and became a youth coach at Walsall.

FACT 87
2007
HALFTIME
CARDIAC ARREST

Leicester City's League Cup tie at Nottingham Forest on 28th August 2007 was abandoned at half time when Clive Clarke suffered a cardiac arrest.

Clarke had recently joined City on loan from Sunderland. He collapsed in the changing rooms at halftime of a game that the Foxes were losing 1-0. He was taken to hospital and the game was abandoned.

By the end of the night the BBC was able to report that Clarke's condition had stabilised but that he would be kept in overnight. He later recalled having been involved in a collision, feeling a bit queasy and then passing out.

When the two sides met again in the rearranged fixture, City's players sportingly allowed Forest to walk the ball into the net from kick-off so the game could resume at 1-0. Forest were unable to seize this initiative however and City hit back to win 3-2.

Clarke returned to Sunderland and remained hopeful of resuming his career. However in February 2008 he retired from playing after seeking medical advice. He returned to his native Ireland and became a football agent.

FACT 88
2008
RELEGATED TO
THE THIRD TIER

2007-08 was a disastrous season for Leicester City. They had three managers and were relegated to the third tier for the first time in their history.

Martin Allen was appointed in the close season but resigned after just three league games, citing interference by chairman Milan Mandaric. Gary Megson came in, but after just six weeks he left to take over at Premier League Bolton. Frank Burrows and Gerry Taggart took temporary charge for a month and when Ian Holloway was appointed in late November, City were seventeenth in the table.

Although they continued to struggle, the Foxes' destiny was always in their own hands. Safety could have been assured with victory in their penultimate game at home to fellow strugglers Sheffield Wednesday. However a 3-1 defeat meant they knew the only way of guaranteeing survival would be if they could win at promotion chasing Stoke City on the last day.

Despite their best efforts, City could only draw 0-0 at Stoke and were relegated due to Southampton's win over Sheffield United. Leicester's proud record of being one of just nine teams to have remained in the top two divisions was over. A few weeks after the season ended Holloway left the club by mutual consent.

FACT 89
2009
RECORD BREAKING SEASON IN THIRD TIER

Leicester City's stay in the third tier was brief and memorable. They finished the season as champions of League One, breaking several club records along the way.

Under new manager Nigel Pearson the Foxes had a good start, picking up ten points from the first twelve available. They then lost at home to Millwall but responded with four straight wins. October was not a good month with three wins and a defeat, but City remained in the playoff positions.

On 1st November City scored two late goals to beat Bristol Rovers 2-1 at home. This acted as a springboard for the rest of the campaign. They remained unbeaten for 23 games and lost just two more all season.

Promotion and the championship was secured with two games to spare as Matty Fryatt scored twice in a 2-0 win at Southend on 19th April. Fryatt finished the season with 32 goals in all competitions, the first City player to get more than thirty since Arthur Riley in the 1950s.

City ended the 46 game season with 27 wins, four defeats and 96 points. They were all club records although the number of wins and points were broken again in 2014.

FACT 90
2010
SVEN GORAN ERIKSSON

Leicester City pulled off something of a managerial coup in November 2010 by appointing Sven Goran Eriksson, but things failed to work out for him at the club.

After nine games of the season City were bottom of the Championship. Paulo Sousa, who had only been in charge since the summer, was sacked by new owners Asia Football Investments and just three days later Eriksson was appointed.

The Swede had won domestic and continental honours in Sweden, Portugal and Italy and also taken England to the World Cup quarter finals. He quickly turned fortunes round and the Foxes climbed out of the relegation zone and up the table. Even a push for the playoffs looked possible but eventually they had to settle for tenth.

During the summer of 2011 Eriksson was given significant backing in the transfer market, but the side had an inconsistent start to the season. After just five wins in the opening thirteen games he left by mutual consent, the board feeling he did not have enough experience at Championship level.

Martin O'Neill was widely tipped to return to the club but in the end it was another former manager who was appointed. Little more than a year after leaving to take over at Hull City, Nigel Pearson was back at Leicester.

FACT 91
2013 PLAY OFF HEARTBREAK

2012-13 was a topsy turvy season for Leicester City. After looking set for automatic promotion they ended up only just making the playoffs, then lost the semi-final in heart-breaking fashion.

The Foxes were in second place at the end of January, but a run of just one win in twelve games saw them drop down to eighth with four games remaining. On the last day of the regular season their fate was out of their hands. As well as needing to win at Nottingham Forest, who were also in contention, they needed Bolton to slip up.

An injury time goal by Anthony Knockaert secured a 3-2 win for City, their first at Forest since 1972. Bolton's failure to beat Blackpool meant City took the last playoff spot and faced a two-legged semi-final with Watford.

At the King Power, David Nugent's late goal gave City a narrow lead to take into the second leg. Deep into injury time at Vicarage Road with City trailing 2-1 Knockaert was fouled and a penalty was awarded. He stepped up to take it but the kick and rebound were saved, then from the counter-attack Troy Deeney scored for the home side. City's dreams of a Premier League return had been dashed in the cruellest manner.

FACT 92
2014
A JOINT RECORD
7th SECOND TIER TITLE

Leicester City were promoted back to the Premier League in 2013-14. They did so as champions of England's second tier for a record seventh time, as well as setting a number of club bests.

City made their intentions clear by taking ten points out of the first twelve available. They went top of the table on Boxing Day and stayed there, losing just once more all season. Between December and February they won a club record nine games in succession. Their total 31 wins that season was also a club record.

Promotion was secured on the first weekend in April. On the Friday night the Foxes beat Sheffield Wednesday 2-1 at home, then on the Saturday defeats for QPR and Derby County meant they couldn't be caught. The title was clinched at Bolton on 22nd April when there were still two more games remaining.

City finished the season with 102 points, their highest ever total. They also scored in a club record 31 consecutive games and had their highest ever total of home wins (seventeen) and away league games unbeaten (thirteen).

In winning the title, City were champions of the second tier for a joint record seventh time, a record they share with Manchester City.

FACT 93
2015
LEICESTER CITY'S
OLDEST PLAYER

Goalkeeper Mark Schwarzer became both Leicester City's oldest debutant and player in 2015. He then went on to break the oldest player record in each of his seven further appearances for the club.

An Australian international with over 100 caps, Schwarzer was best known for making over 500 appearances for Middlesbrough and Fulham. He then spent two and a half seasons as a backup keeper at Chelsea before joining City in January 2015 to provide cover for the injured Kasper Schmeichel.

On 24th January Schwarzer made his debut against Tottenham Hotspur in an FA Cup fourth round tie at White Hart Lane. He was 42 years and 111 days old. The following week he kept goal in a 3-1 defeat against Manchester United in the Premier League at Old Trafford. By the end of the season he had made six league appearances as City avoided relegation.

Schwarzer remained at the Foxes for 2015-16. He didn't make any appearances in the historic title winning season but did make three appearances in the League Cup. The last of these was on 27th October against Hull City, when he was 43 years and 21 days old. He was released from the club at the end of the season and retired from playing.

FACT 94
2015
THE GREAT ESCAPE

Leicester City looked certainties for relegation at the beginning of April 2015. They then won seven games out of nine to survive, but it wasn't enough to save manager Nigel Pearson from the sack.

Defeat at Tottenham on 21st March left City rooted to the bottom of the table, where they had been since November. Going into an international break, they were seven points from safety and without a win in eight games.

When domestic action resumed, Leicester won four games in succession to move out of the relegation zone. A 3-1 home defeat to eventual champions Chelsea didn't disrupt City's rhythm and they picked up ten points from the last three games to finish fourteenth, six points above the drop zone.

It came as a surprise at the end of June, just days before pre-season training, that Pearson was dismissed. A club statement said that there were "fundamental differences in perspective between him and the board."

Two weeks later 63-year-old Italian Claudio Ranieri was appointed as Pearson's successor. He had managed Chelsea from 2000 to 2004 but recently been sacked by Greece after losing at home to the Faroe Islands. Club legend Gary Lineker was not impressed, calling him an "uninspired choice". He would be proved wrong in spectacular fashion.

FACT 95

2015
JAMIE VARDY'S SCORING RECORD

In the first half of Leicester City's amazing 2015-16 title winning season, Jamie Vardy set a record by scoring in eleven consecutive Premier League games in the same campaign.

Vardy's run started with a late penalty at Bournemouth on 29th August. The following day the striker who was playing non-league football just four years earlier was called up to the England squad for the first time.

He then scored in each of the next nine games. These included an injury time equaliser in a 2-2 draw at Southampton and a penalty whilst playing with a broken wrist bone against Norwich. On 21st November he scored in a 3-0 win at Newcastle that took the Foxes to the top of the league.

By scoring in ten successive games, Vardy had equalled a record set by Manchester United's Ruud Van Nistelrooy in 2003. Ironically, United were City's next opponents at the King Power Stadium.

There was an electric atmosphere on 28th November, when both sides sought to go above Manchester City at the top of the table. In the 24th minute the stadium erupted when Vardy ran on to Christian Fuchs' long ball to score with a powerful low shot.

Although United equalised just before halftime, nobody could take Vardy's record away from him and there were greater things to come in 2016.

FACT 96

2016
5,000-1
CHAMPIONS

Leicester City completed what is arguably the greatest upset in sporting history when they won the Premier League in 2015-16.

Prior to the start of the season City were 5,000-1 with some bookmakers to win the Premier League. Although they were unbeaten in their first six games, many predicted a 5-2 home defeat to Arsenal would start a spiral down the table.

City responded brilliantly, taking 26 points out of the next thirty available. They were top of the league at Christmas and although they wobbled slightly, their only win in five games was a crucial 1-0 victory at fellow title hopefuls Tottenham.

In the first week of February City beat Liverpool and Manchester City to go five points clear. They then lost at Arsenal to a last-minute goal but were only galvanized more and didn't lose again.

By April only Tottenham could realistically overhaul the Foxes. The Londoners buckled though and on the evening of 2nd May they threw away a 2-0 lead at Chelsea. It meant Leicester City were champions of England.

There were memorable scenes at the King Power Stadium on 7th May when the players paraded the trophy after beating Everton 3-1. Nine days later, a quarter of a million turned out for an open topped bus parade. Claudio Ranieri and his players had achieved the impossible.

FACT 97
2017 CHAMPIONS LEAGUE QUARTER FINALISTS

Leicester City's first appearance in the Champions League saw them reach the quarter-final, where they were beaten by Atletico Madrid.

The Foxes progressed comfortably to the knockout stages, finishing top of a group that also contained Porto, Bruges and Copenhagen. The round of sixteen saw City paired with Sevilla, winners of the Europa League in 2016.

In the first leg at the Sanchez Pizjuan stadium, City trailed 2-0 but a crucial goal from Jamie Vardy seventeen minutes from time gave them hope for the return game. The following day, Claudio Ranieri was sensationally sacked with the Foxes struggling in the Premier League and Craig Shakespeare put in temporary charge.

On an unforgettable night at the King Power, goals from Wes Morgan and Marc Allbrighton gave City a 2-0 lead. Despite being down to ten men, Sevilla didn't give up and City were thankful to Kasper Schmeichel who saved a penalty.

City faced La Liga opposition again in the quarter finals, being drawn against Atletico Madrid. The Foxes lost 1-0 in Spain but there was to be no turnaround at the King Power. Saul scored for Atletico in the first half and although Vardy equalised with half an hour to go, City couldn't find the two more goals needed to go through.

FACT 98

2018 HELICOPTER TRAGEDY

Tragedy struck Leicester City on 27th October 2018 when club owner Vichai Srivaddhanaprabha and four others were killed when his helicopter crashed shortly after take-off from the King Power stadium.

The sight of Vichai's helicopter on the pitch after games was a common one. It took off less than ninety minutes after City had drawn 1-1 with West Ham United and earlier BT Sport cameras had shown it preparing for the trip.

After the pilot had turned the helicopter a tail rotor linkage broke, sending it into an uncontrollable spin. It crashed in a club car park 200 metres from the stadium, bursting into flames. There was no chance of survival for anybody on board, with police officers who ran to the scene having to retreat due to the intense heat.

The others who died were two members of Vichai's staff, the pilot and co-pilot. There were still plenty of fans in the vicinity and it was a miracle nobody on the ground was killed. The following day, scarves, shirts and flowers were left at the stadium by devastated fans.

Vichai's body was repatriated to Thailand for a traditional Buddhist funeral. The Foxes Foundation was renamed the Vichai Srivaddhanaprabha Foundation in his honour. His son Aiyawatt took control of the club, vowing to continue with his father's vision and dreams.

FACT 99
2019
TOP FLIGHT
RECORD AWAY WIN

On 25th October 2019 Leicester City thrashed Southampton 9-0 at St Mary's Stadium, becoming the first English team to win by nine goals away from home in the top-flight.

Ben Chilwell gave the Foxes a tenth minute lead, then soon afterwards Southampton were reduced to ten men when Ryan Bertrand was sent off. Youri Tielemans doubled the lead after seventeen minutes and two minutes later Ayoze Perez got the third.

Perez added another in the 39th minute and shortly before halftime Jamie Vardy scored City's fifth. After the break there was no let up, Perez and Vardy scoring within a minute of each other to make it 7-0 after an hour.

With five minutes remaining James Maddison scored the eighth from a free kick. In the fourth minute of injury time, City were awarded a penalty when Vardy was fouled in the area by Jan Bednarek. Vardy dusted himself down to convert the kick himself to complete his own hat-trick and a 9-0 rout.

The emphatic scoreline equalled a Premier League record also held by Manchester United. It was also the biggest margin of victory away from home by any side in top-flight English football since the formation of the Football League in 1888.

FACT 100

2020 C.L. QUALIFICATION AGONY

In the 2019-20 season that was disrupted by the Coronavirus pandemic Leicester looked set for Champions League qualification, only to lose out on the final day.

Eight successive wins between October and December lifted the Foxes into second place. However they remained some way off runaway leaders Liverpool, who won 4-0 at the King Power Stadium on Boxing Day to move thirteen points clear.

Although Manchester City would move up to second in January, a 4-0 home win over Aston Villa on 9th March 2020 kept the Foxes in third place and firmly on course for Champions League qualification with nine games to go. However later that week the Premier League was suspended due to the worsening situation with the pandemic.

When it was deemed safe to return to playing in June, the government insisted that all fixtures took place behind closed doors. City resumed with disappointing draws against relegation threatened Watford and Brighton, followed by a defeat at Everton.

Despite just two wins in eight games since the restart, qualification for the Champions League was in City's hands on the last day of the season. Victory over Manchester United at the King Power would lift them above United into the top four. However a 2-0 defeat meant they would have to settle for the Europa League in 2020-21.

The 100 Facts Series

Arsenal, *Steve Horton*	978-1-908724-09-0
Aston Villa, *Steve Horton*	978-1-908724-98-4
Celtic, *Steve Horton*	978-1-908724-10-6
Chelsea, *Kristian Downer*	978-1-908724-11-3
Everton, *Bob Sharp*	978-1-908724-12-0
Hearts, *Steve Horton*	978-1-912782-48-2
Leeds, *Steve Horton*	978-1-908724-94-6
Leicester City, *Steve Horton*	978-1-912782-47-5
Liverpool, *Steve Horton*	978-1-908724-13-7
Manchester City, *Steve Horton*	978-1-908724-14-4
Manchester United, *Iain McCartney*	978-1-908724-15-1
Newcastle United, *Steve Horton*	978-1-908724-16-8
Norwich City, *Steve Horton*	978-1-908724-99-1
Nottingham Forest, *Steve Horton*	978-1-912782-46-8
Rangers, *David Clayton*	978-1-908724-17-5
Sheffield United, *Steve Horton*	978-1-912782-45-1
Tottenham Hotspur, *Steve Horton*	978-1-908724-18-2
West Ham, *Steve Horton*	978-1-908724-80-9

Player Autographs

Player Autographs

Player Autographs

Player Autographs

Player Autographs

Player Autographs

Player Autographs